D0856377

Columbia University

Contributions to Education

Teachers College Series

No. 130

AMS PRESS
NEW YORK

MEASUREMENTS OF MECHANICAL ABILITY

BY

JOHN L. STENQUIST, PH.D.

TEACHERS COLLEGE, COLUMBIA UNIVERSITY
CONTRIBUTIONS TO EDUCATION, NO. 130

219481

PUBLISHED BY
Teachers College, Columbia University
NEW YORK CITY
1923

Library of Congress Cataloging in Publication Data

Stenquist, John Langdon, 1885-1952.
  Measurements of mechanical ability.

  Reprint of the 1923 ed., issued in series: Teachers
College, Columbia University. Contributions to edu-
cation, no. 130.
  Originally presented as the author's thesis, Columbia.

  1. Mechanical ability--Testing. I. Title.
II. Series: Columbia University. Teachers College.
Contributions to education, no. 130.
LB1139.M4S7 1972   153.9'324   73-177744
ISBN 0-404-55130-0

Reprinted by Special Arrangement with Teachers
College Press, New York, New York

From the edition of 1923, New York
First AMS edition published in 1972
Manufactured in the United States

AMS PRESS, INC.
NEW YORK, N. Y.   10003

ACKNOWLEDGMENTS

To Professor E. L. Thorndike, who is at once the inspiration and guiding genius of all who are so fortunate as to be associated with him, is chiefly due whatever merit this study may have, and grateful acknowledgment is here made of my great indebtedness to him. Very great credit is also due Professor H. A. Ruger for his unfailing personal interest and constant helpful counsel. Professor W. A. McCall has given much help in the statistical treatment of the data. To the principal, assistant principals, and shop teachers of Public School No. 64, Manhattan, credit is also due for coöperation in the giving of many tests.

J. L. S.

CONTENTS

PART I

A Description of the Tests *

---

* The Mechanical Assembling Tests herein described may be obtained from Chas. Stoelting Co., 3037 Carroll Ave., Chicago.

The Picture Tests of Mechanical Aptitude are published by the World Book Co., Yonkers, N. Y.

TABLES

FIGURES

PART I

Section I

Introductory

THIS study presents descriptions, results, and conclusions resulting from experiments with mechanical tests carried on over a period of four or five years. The important feature is probably that it deals mainly with a new type of test material, namely, common mechanical articles of everyday life adapted for use as tests under standardized conditions. In addition to this, however, are the results obtained in the use of picture tests dealing with similar mechanical objects, and mechanical situations, designed to test mechanical information, aptitude and ability.

Little has thus far been done to make mental tests less academic and verbal, despite the great interest that has sprung up in the general field. Yet it is well known that a large percentage of the population is ill adapted by nature and by training to excel in the verbal, pencil-and-paper tasks that are imposed by the average mental test. By general agreement many of these are called measures of general intelligence, but it is certain that many abilities which could well be termed general are not measured by them. Any means of examining into the more or less unexplored abilities otherwise not reached is therefore important and this has been the guiding notion in the present research.

The tests described touch but a small portion of mechanical activities that can be tested, but within their range they are believed to be significant. They deal specifically with the world of objects,—real things, as distinguished from words, and involve both mechanical skill and abstract mental ability. While their nature is essentially mechanical they are in no sense trade tests, but should rather be considered tests of general mechanical intelligence and manual aptitude. The picture tests do not, of course, test skill in the sense of providing objects for manipulation, but the ability to answer the problems correlates well with such skills.

I

But the use of actual objects or mechanical devices as test material involves disadvantages as well as advantages,—disadvantages in that physical objects are always more cumbersome to handle and to manage than printed forms. They are more expensive and require more time to use; they involve various minor difficulties, such as differences in supposedly identical articles due to minor details; such, for example, as the differing tension or stiffness of supposedly identical springs, etc. Models also wear out, are broken, bent or otherwise spoiled.

The importance of measuring this ability, however, far outweighs the obstacles met in the mere nature of the materials. It is well to keep in mind that modern life is permeated with machines and mechanical devices on every hand, and that the ability to handle them is daily becoming more and more important to every one. We should also keep in mind that while but a small fraction of the population is engaged in the *manufacture* of this multitude of devices and machines, every individual in modern civilized life is concerned directly or indirectly with their uses. Ability in this direction is therefore of increasing importance.

The past two or three decades have forced recognition of the importance of the general field of manual or industrial education and there is now scarcely a school that does not make some provision, no matter how inadequate, for manual work. An increasing number of elementary schools also now provide so-called prevocational courses for pupils above the 6th grade. The choice or rejection of mechanical courses by the average boy is apt to be on the flimsiest grounds, and it is here that standardized tests of general mechanical aptitude will be useful. Enormous differences are found among children of the same age or grade and it is believed that tests, such as those herein described, will prove useful in more intelligent, educational and vocational guidance of pupils.

No claim is made that the whole problem of measuring mechanical ability has been solved,—only that a small but specific contribution has been made. In the use of these tests, as in the use of all others, it is necessary to continually counsel the need of careful interpretation of results obtained, liberal use of common sense, and due consideration of all other factors involved.

SECTION II

TESTS OF GENERAL MECHANICAL ABILITY

DEFINITIONS OF TERMS; NATURE OF TESTS USED

The term Mechanical Ability as here used means general aptitude in the management and manipulation of things mechanical. It implies a general knowledge of mechanical principles and usages, but does not imply any special trade skill. The tests described have been designed to measure the general mechanical ability of young people of school age, who have learned no trade, but who may have much or little potential ability of this kind.

Possibly it would be more appropriate to designate these tests by some other name for they are mechanical only in a limited sense. The only mechanical *skill* involved is that of assembling, and this is, as every one knows, but a small part of the multitude of mechanical skills. On the mental side they call for the ability to recognize parts of ordinary mechanical devices, for the ability to make judgments as to the reasons for the particular size, shape, weight and nature of the parts,—in short, for the mental ability to think through in some degree the same steps as those employed by the designer of each machine. Manually, they call for the dexterity required to put parts together to form the completed machine or device after it has been decided how they should go. Much of the performance of a typical child is, of course, mere trial and error manipulation, in which he hopes somehow to make the thing work. But the nature of the various models is such that only a very low score is possible for the individual who depends merely upon thoughtless manipulation of the parts. A generous amount of the best kind of thinking is thus required to make a high score. It involves accurate perception, reasoning and judgment, applied to each model. In so far, therefore, as these mental processes are of general importance in everyday life the ability demonstrated in assembling these models perfectly could well be called general intelligence. But since this term has been largely accepted as meaning a more abstract ability, it is not thought advisable to refer to these tests as general intelligence measures, but rather as tests of the general mechanical ability here described.

Two general kinds of materials have been tried: 1. Assembling tests, in which actual disassembled objects are put together. 2. Picture tests, calling for judgments as to what parts belong together, and including questions on mechanics and machines.

The idea of presenting a disassembled actual commercial article, such, for example, as a bicycle bell or mouse trap to be assembled, was first suggested by Professor E. L. Thorndike as a promising method of reaching certain capacities more or less untouched by the more common verbal pencil-and-paper tests. In order to make them practicable as group tests in schools only such models as can be given to whole groups of pupils have been included. To meet this requirement it has been necessary that all models be relatively small, light and unbreakable, so that they can easily be carried about and used over and over, as well as that they be of such a nature that they can be readily disassembled or assembled. The final Single Series herein described probably represents the best types of models. They can be quickly and positively scored, and easily disassembled by boys after taking the test.

While it would be desirable to include other operations besides assembling, this one activity was chosen as representative of many mechanical tasks and calls less for special trade skill than most mechanical operations. Thus, assembling is of a more general nature than, e.g., chiselling, chipping, filing, sawing, soldering, forging, etc., all of which require at least some trade training.

The picture tests, however, cover a much wider range of objects and operations, and include questions pertaining not only to simple and small objects but to large and complicated machines and processes.

FIG. 1.   Original Series I.

SECTION III

DESCRIPTION OF ASSEMBLING TESTS—ORIGINAL SERIES I

The first test tried consisted of seven very common mechanical contrivances placed in a corrugated cardboard box, 16 by 16 by 2 inches, which could be placed on an ordinary school desk. This has been generally called the "Stenquist Construction Test," Original Series I.[1] Fig. 1 shows its essential nature.

1. MODELS INCLUDED IN SERIES I

The objects placed in the box were:

2 Carriage bolts with nuts, $\frac{3}{8}$ by 3 inches.
2 Pieces of safety chain containing 10 links.
2 Small bicycle monkey wrenches.
2 Round wooden mouse traps.
2 Models made of three angle irons bolted together with screws.
2 Small rim locks.
2 Bicycle bells.

In the upper compartment was placed one complete set of the models, fully assembled. In the lower half was placed an exact duplicate set, completely disassembled.

The task consists in assembling each model as rapidly and perfectly as possible.

2. METHOD OF GIVING AND SCORING

Twenty-four children were arranged, one in a seat, in an ordinary classroom. After a record blank had been filled out, the following instructions were given: "Lay the paper which you have just filled out on top of your desk near one edge where you can get it easily later." The twenty-four boxes containing the test materials were then distributed. Holding up one of the

---

[1] This test is described also in Stenquist, J. L., Thorndike, E. L., Trabue, M. R., "The Intellectual Status of Children Who are Public Charges," Archives of Psychology, No. 33, published by Department of Psychology, Columbia University.

boxes before them, directions were given as follows: "Turn the box which you have on your desk so that the letter 'F' is toward you.[1] Do not look into the box till I say go.[2]

"Each of these boxes is divided into two parts (indicating by gesture how the partition extended across the middle of the box). In the compartment or part farthest away from you there are seven mechanical models, i.e., seven mechanical things; one of them is a bolt with a nut on it; another is a small wrench; another a small chain; and there are four other things.

"In the part nearest to you there are seven mechanical things just like the others except these are all taken apart. I want you to take all the parts in the compartment nearest you and make seven mechanical things exactly like the ones in the compartment farthest away from you as quickly as you can. As soon as you have finished them all, raise your hand; and we will write on your record sheet just how long it took you to do them all.

"Begin with the one that looks the easiest.

"If you want to take apart any of the models to see how they are made you may do so, but you must put them together again. Screw all the nuts up tight; don't leave them half on, but don't use the wrench to tighten them with. Do you understand?" (Repeated if necessary.)

"You will now get ready. Grasp the sides of the box so that you can take the cover off quickly when I tell you to. Are you all ready? Go!"

The instructions being somewhat long, we found it necessary after the children began to work to give also the following instructions. This was done after three minutes:

"Do the ones that you think are the easiest first. Screw all nuts up tight with your fingers but do not use the wrench."

We found that two examiners could manage twenty-four subjects. As soon as a hand was raised, the examiner noted the time from his stop-watch, walked over and entered it on the record sheet of that pupil. The pupil then replaced everything in the box and put his record sheet in the box ready to be graded.

At the end of 30 minutes all children were required to stop work.

---

[1] "F" means front.
[2] We found it necessary to be very vigilant in keeping the subjects from opening the boxes before the signal was given, as the pressure of curiosity became very great.

3. RESULTS

The pupil's achievement with each of the seven models was graded on a basis of 0 to 10, by an arbitrary schedule of partial score values. All perfect scores were given 10 points each. All seven models assembled perfectly in the full 30 minutes then gave a score of 10 × 7, or 70. An arbitrary value of 1 was given every "gain-minute," i.e., for every minute of the 30 that remained after the pupil had completed the test. For example, if the subject completed the test in 16 minutes, 12 seconds, 14 points were added to his score. Fractions less than one-half minute were neglected. Fractions of more than one-half minute were counted as 1.

We found that after a little practice, and with skilled management of boy helpers, one examiner and four boy helpers can grade the twenty-four sets in about 40 minutes.

We had then for each child a record like the following sample:

Pupil	Score Attained with Each Model							Credit for Time	Total Score
	A	B	C	D	E	F	G		
1.............	10	10	4	3	0	0	0	0	27
2.............	10	10	10	10	10	10	3	0	63
3.............	10	10	10	10	10	10	10	8	78

2

Section IV

Measures of 697 Children in Mechanical Ability

Although the results obtained with this series, Original Series I, have, as already indicated (page 5), been reported elsewhere, the essential facts are here repeated for the sake of making this account complete.

SCORES OF NORMAL CHILDREN

The test was first given to 432 unselected children in a New York City public school, and the scores tabulated as shown in Table I to yield age norms.

From these norms true norms were estimated to be as follows:

	Age									
	6 to 7	7 to 8	8 to 9	9 to 10	10 to 11	11 to 12	12 to 13	13 to 14	14 to 15	15 to 16
Median Score.....	34.5	33.75	42.5	51.25	59.3	62.5	66.78	76.4	77.5	82.5
Estimated True Score..........	20	32	42	50	57	63	69	75	79	82

The discrepancies between the obtained and estimated medians are due to the allowance made for especially bright six- and seven-year children.

Having these norms the real work of the first experiment was begun, namely, to measure the ability of 265 children who were in institutions for dependent children. Four tests were given—Binet, Trabue Language, Thorndike Reading, and this mechanical test.

By utilizing the median score for ages 6, 7, 8, etc., and interpolating the scores for each intervening month, a table of age norms was built up. It was then only necessary to read the table to determine the degree of over-ageness or under-ageness of any child subsequently measured. (Since the test in this original form has been discontinued the table is not here reproduced.)

TABLE I

FREQUENCIES OF SCORES ATTAINED BY 432 ORDINARY CHILDREN AS TESTED IN A PUBLIC SCHOOL OF NEW YORK CITY—ARRANGED BY AGES

6 = 6.0 up to 7; 7 = 7.0 up to 8, etc.

Score	Age										
	6	7	8	9	10	11	12	13	14	15	16
4.....		I									
5.....		I									
6.....		I									
7.....		I									
8.....	I		I								
9.....											
10.....	I		I								
11.....		I									
12.....											
13.....		2	2								
14.....		2	2								
15.....	I	I			I						
16.....		I		I							
17.....		2									
18.....		I									
19.....		I			I						
20.....		I	I	I							
21.....		2									
22.....	I	3	3		I			I			
23.....		I		I	2	I					
24.....	2	I	I	I							
25.....		I	3		2		I				
26.....	2		2		I						
27.....		4	I			2					
28.....	8	I		2	I						
29.....			2								
30.....	I	2	I	I							
31.....		I	I	I							
32.....		I	I	I							
33.....			3								
34.....			I			I					
35.....			I	2	I	I					
36.....	2	2		I	3						
37.....	2	2	I			I		I			
38.....				I	3		I				
39.....		I	I								

TABLE I—*Cont'd.*

Score	Age										
	6	7	8	9	10	11	12	13	14	15	16
40.....		I	I	I	4			I			
41.....			I			I	2				
42.....				3		2					
43.....		I	5	I		5	I	2			
44.....		2	I	4	I	I					
45.....		I	2	3	I					I	
46.....	I	3	I					I	I		
47.....	I	I	I		I			I			
48.....	I	2	2	3	2	I	2				
49.....		2	2	I	I						
50.....		I	2	2				I			
51.....	I	I			I	I					
52.....			I	6	I	I					
53.....			I		2			3			
54.....			2				I	I			
55.....	I	I	I	I	2	2		I	I		
56.....	I	I	I	I	3	I		I		I	
57.....		2		2	I						
58.....			I	2	I	2		I			
59.....			2			2					
60.....		I	3	I	I		I		I		
61.....			I	I	2						
62.....			I	I	I				I		
63.....			I	3	3	2					
64.....		I		I	3	2	I				
65.....				I	I	2	2				
66.....		2			I						
67.....			4	I	3						
68.....			I	I	2	I	I				
69.....				2	3	I					
70.....				2	I	I		I			
71.....				I	I	2		I	I	3	
72.....				2		I	I				
73.....					I		I		I		
74.....							I	I			
75.....					2	I		3			
76.....						2	I	I		I	
77.....					3	I		I	I		
78.....			I		3		I	I	3		

TABLE I—*Cont'd.*

Score	Age										
	6	7	8	9	10	11	12	13	14	15	16
79.....						I		I		I	
80.....				I	2		2	3	I		
81.....							I	I		I	
82.....				I	I	6		2	I	I	
83.....						I	I			I	
84.....			I			I		2	2	I	
85.....					I	2		I			
86.....					I					I	
87.....								2			
88.....						I		3		4	
89.....								I			
90.....									I		
91.....									I		
92.....											I

Section V

Results and Conclusions from the First Experiment

As a measuring device the experiment demonstrated the practicability of utilizing such materials as have been described. The interest displayed by the children was intense, and even those children who were almost complete failures at it were anxious to try. The test as a whole proved too easy (the more able finishing within 10 minutes with perfect scores) and hence was probably unreliable for individual deductions, but general averages are sufficiently reliable. The marked differences between the type of ability measured by the mechanical test and the abstract intellect tests is significant. The records of 50 boys and 50 girls selected at random from the total results for all the dependent children are reproduced in Table II.

The results show that the dependent children are as a group about $1\frac{3}{4}$ years behind in mechanical ability, but considerably more so in abstract intellectual ability. The 11- and 12-year-olds are about 2 years behind; the 13- and 14-year-olds about $2\frac{1}{2}$ years; and the 15-and 16-year-olds about $4\frac{1}{2}$ years behind.

But the pupils behind in abstract ability are not always behind in mechanical ability.

The percentage of unlike signed deviations is for the cases cited about .31, which is equivalent to a correlation of but about .5. Pupil 29, e.g., is 1.8 years behind in abstract ability but 3.3 years ahead in mechanical ability. Correlations with subsequent and more perfected mechanical tests show that the true correlation between intelligence tests and the mechanical tests is seldom over .4. Thus it is confirmed that a pupil *may* be inferior in academic school work and yet have marked ability in manual activities. But there is no evidence to support the popular notion of a law of compensation,—which assumes that low abstract intellect signifies high mechanical ability, or vice versa. Our correlations are low—but always *positive*—between the two abilities. If we know that a pupil is above average in abstract ability all we can predict with regard to his mechanical ability is that he is more likely to be

12

TABLE II

ILLUSTRATIVE RESULTS WITH ORIGINAL SERIES I

BOYS

Identification Number	Age Used in Computing Under-Ageness Estimates	Under-Ageness in Three Tests of Abstract Intellect Combined. (+ Equals Over-Ageness)	Under-Ageness in Mechanical Test. (+ Equals Over-Ageness)
1	14.2	—2.7	—8.7
2	12.7	— .1	+2.1
3	10.0	—1.3	+4.5
4	13.8	—3.0	—3.0
5	10.4	+ .1	—1.5
6	10.2	—1.1	—2.9
7	9.8	+ .4	+3.4
8	14.?	— .8	....
9	9.8	—1.8	—3.1
10	12.2	.0	+1.4
11	11.2	+1.1	— .8
12	14.0	—3.1	—2.2
13	14.1	—1.6	+1.1
14	12.3	—1.2	+2.3
15	12.?	—2.7	....
16	13.?	+ .2	....
17	13.8	+1.8	—1.3
18	10.7	—1.6	—1.4
19	12.7	—2.7	—1.0
20	12.7	—1.1	+ .3
21	10.3	+ .1	+1.3
22	13.6	— .3	+3.4
23	9.9	+ .1	+3.5
24	15.2	— .9	— .4
25	12.8	—2.9	....
26	12.7	—2.4	....
27	14.?	—3.0	....
28	11.0	— .3	—3.4
29	13.0	—1.8	+3.3
30	13.?	—3.9	—3.1
31	14.3	—2.5	....
32	13.9	—3.3	....
33	16.6	—3.3	+ .7
34	10.?	—2.1	....
35	10.9	— .5	+ .4
36	11.2	+ .3	— .9
37	12.0	+1.3	+2.3
38	10.5	—1.0	—3.6
39	9.8	—1.8	—1.5
40	10.0	—2.5	—2.7
41	13.2	+1.9	—1.5
42	14.3	—2.4	—1.3
43	10.5	— .1	—2.7
44	12.4	—2.1	—2.1
45	14.0	+ .6	—1.2
46	14.?	— .4	....
47	10.4	+ .2	—2.6
48	13.2	—3.9	—1.6
49	10.9	—1.5	—2.2
50	10.3	—1.2	— .6

TABLE II—(Cont'd)

GIRLS

Identification Number	Age Used in Computing Under-Ageness Estimates	Under-Ageness in Three Tests of Abstract Intellect Combined. (+ Equals Over-Ageness)	Under-Ageness in Mechanical Test. (+ Equals Over-Ageness)
200	10.5	+ .4	—1.2
201	15.2	—4.1	—3.8
202	11.8	—1.0	—2.1
203	13.8	—1.9	—2.1
204	10.2	— .5	—1.3
205	11.2	—2.0	—4.2
206	14.3	— .6	+ .2
207	12.4	—2.5	—3.4
208	9.0	— .6	—3.5
209	11.5	—1.5	—5.5
210	14.2	—5.0	—7.6
211	15.3	—5.8	—3.6
212	12.0	—1.7	—3.0
213	10.7	—1.9	—2.7
214	13.1	—4.3	—4.8
215	10.7	—2.6	—3.1
216	11.6	— .6	—4.1
217	13.2	—3.8	— .4
218	9.1	— .5	—2.3
219	9.4	— .2	—1.3
220	11.0	— .5	—2.7
221	13.0	—2.8	—2.5
222	14.8	— .1	—1.0
223	9.4	+ .7	—1.3
224	11.2	—2.8	— .2
225	10.?	—2.0	....
226	14.4	—2.8	—1.7
227	14.3	+ .2	+ .2
228	12.9	—3.2	—3.6
229	9.8	— .3	—1.5
230	10.2	— .8	—3.1
231	12.1	+1.4	—3.1
232	11.2	—2.9	—5.4
233	8.?	— .6	....
234	11.8	—1.2	—4.0
235	14.5	—3.3	—1.3
236	10.8	—1.7	— .4
237	12.0	+1.2	—5.6
238	9.0	— .7	+1.5
239	11.8	—2.4	—1.8
240	9.8	+2.8	+1.7
241	10.2	—2.4	—5.2
242	13.4	—1.3	+1.1
243	9.8	+ .4	.0
244	11.9	—3.9	+5.2
245	11.1	—3.0	—5.4
246	11.?	+2.3	....
247	13.?	+1.0	....
248	11.2	+ .2	—3.6
249	12.4	—3.5	— .9
250	9.9	+1.5	—1.3

above average in it also, but there are many chances for him to be below. It is clear that mechanical ability is not measured by ordinary paper mental tests and that it is worth while to further develop the type of test materials here tried out.

With this in mind a second series of models was accordingly designed and tried out. This series is called Original Series II.

Section VI

Construction of Assembling Test—Original Series II

Experience with Series I indicated the need for a series of more difficult models, in order that the test might be extended upward into high school and college grades, and also the desirability of more substantial boxes. Accordingly, after much search for suitable models six considerably more difficult than Series I were selected. These are shown in Fig. 2, together with the improved box.

1. MODELS INCLUDED IN SERIES II

The models are:

Model H. Two straps buckled together in a complicated way with two buckles, four slides and two rings.

Model I. A wall electric switch.

Model J. A large rim lock.

Model K. An ordinary electric bell.

Model L. The works of a pendulum clock.

Model M. An electric light socket.

As in the case of Series I, a duplicate model not fully assembled was included so that the problem here, as in Series I, was frankly one of copying each model by building up a second model from the parts. In this series each assembled model, together with all the parts of one disassembled model, was placed in a separate compartment provided in the special reversed box, and not mixed as in Series I.

This improvement eliminated the miscellaneous sorting of parts, although, of course, it also eliminated that feature of the test which called for identification of the particular parts of each model out of the entire mass of parts. But this sorting process, while no doubt a valuable test in itself (later tried out in a different way—see Recognition Test, page 21) was not the kind of reaction which was sought, besides it is wasteful of time. The object

16

here was to test more strictly for manipulative skill. The cover of the box was designed to open toward the person being tested, to form a tray in which to work to avoid losing parts. A large and small screw driver and a pair of tweezers were included in this set. The test was given in the same manner as the preceding Series I, except that at least 50 minutes were found to be necessary.

2. METHOD OF SCORING

The credit given for each model, when perfectly or partially assembled, is shown by the standard score sheet below. After the test the scorer examined each model and entered the score on record sheet which had been signed and placed inside the box by each person examined. The models were then disassembled to be used again. Boys who scored high in the tests were found to be ideal helpers.

CONSTRUCTION OR ASSEMBLING TEST—ORIGINAL SERIES II

STANDARD SCORE SHEET

Grade All Models on a Scale of 0 to 10

MODEL H (STRAP)

	Score	or Deduct
No attempt	0	
Either strap reversed	8	
Both straps reversed	6	
One buckle wrong in any way		3
Loops omitted or wrong, for each		2
Perfect	10	

MODEL I (SWITCH)

No attempt	0	
One contact wrong or omitted		4
Both contacts wrong or omitted	8	
Bracket wrong		3
Perfect	10	

MODEL J (RIM LOCK)

No attempt	0	
Spring loose, not over lug of frame	7	
Spring all wrong or omitted		5
Revolving cam not properly in position with catch	7	
Perfect	10	

Fig. 2. Original Series II.

MODEL K (BELL)

No attempt.. 0
Wires wrong with respect to washers, for each............ 1
For each washer omitted or misplaced................... 1
For omitting or misplacing small square insulations........ 2
For each case of wrong screw used...................... 1
The whole thing about half solved...................... 5

MODEL L (CLOCK)

No attempt.. 0
For works partly assembled: Allow for each pinion in place.... 1
Works all assembled but top frame not in place............ 7
Perfect... 10

MODEL M (SOCKET)

No attempt.. 0
Lower disk inverted.................................. 2
Upper disk inverted.................................. 2
Small nut omitted or misplaced........................ 2
For omitting small black center pin bearing.............. 1
All properly assembled but no tension in spring............ 8

This model frequently occurs in a very mixed-up condition; in such a case judge as to whether the whole effort represents that the problem is one-half, one-fourth or three-fourths solved and grade accordingly.

NOTE—There will be cases where the degree of achievement does not correspond to any of the values given. In this case the obvious procedure is to judge it in terms of the case most like it.

TIME.—The standard time is 50 minutes, although this has been varied.

3. RESULTS

Records were obtained from the following groups, the highest score possible being 60:

	No.	Av.	Time
Freshman engineers, Columbia (1915)...	35	37.4	50 min.
Teachers College graduate students (1915)	29	41.1	60 "
Efficiency men, silk factory (1915).......	30	28.8	42 "
Freshmen, Mass. Institute Technology (1916)............................	40	36.9	48 "
Freshmen and second year, Wentworth Institute (1916)..................	58	43.4	48 "

The results soon demonstrated that the idea of utilizing these very difficult models is impracticable for school purposes. Too much time is consumed in both giving and scoring the material. It is too bulky and awkward to handle in classrooms. It is also difficult to assign proper partial scores to a model that may require 30 minutes and be greatly affected by luck. This series was accordingly never extensively used.

The distribution of scores for 190 cases is shown in Table III:

TABLE III

DISTRIBUTION OF SCORES FOR EACH MODEL

[ORIGINAL SERIES II, IN 190 CASES OF COLLEGE STUDENTS AND OTHER ADULTS]

Model	Score				Total
	0	1–5	6–9	10	
H (Strap)...............	3	7	47	133	190
I (Switch)...............	14	16	14	146	190
J (Lock)................	15	12	62	101	190
K (Electric Bell)..........	19	32	65	74	190
L (Clock)...............	56	24	17	93	190
M (Electric Socket)........	120	29	15	26	190

The order of difficulty is shown to be approximately the order in which the models were arranged in the box, i.e., the order in the table. The frequency of zero scores is exactly in this order. The scores indicated above cannot be taken, however, as entirely reliable for models L and M, as a large number of persons worked so slowly as to leave little or no time to try these models.

The average time required by 35 freshmen engineers per model was as shown in Table IV:

TABLE IV

TIME PER MODEL—35 FRESHMEN ENGINEERS

	H Strap	I Switch	J Lock	K Elec. Bell	L Clock	M Socket
Av. minutes....	7.4	12.5	7.4	12.8	9.2	8.3

A further group of 100 8th grade boys were later examined by Mr. Hazen Chatfield in a New York City public school. From these cases the distribution of each partial score was as shown in Table V:

TABLE V

DISTRIBUTION OF SCORES FOR EACH MODEL, IN 100 CASES OF 8TH GRADE
BOYS OF 11 EXPERT TEACHERS

Score	H Strap	I Switch	J Lock	K Bell	L Clock	M Socket
0...............	8	11	10	16	58	79
1...............	3	3	1	3	3	5
2...............	10	12	6	7	7	5
3...............	1	1	3	8	4	1
4...............	5	5	6	8	5	3
5...............	1	0	6	5	4	2
6...............	1	4	3	4	0	1
7...............	10	6	7	12	2	0
8...............	12	4	7	12	1	0
9...............	9	2	29	13	1	0
10...............	40	52	22	12	15	4
	100	100	100	100	100	100
Approx. Median Scores.........	8.8	10.0	9.0	6.7	0.	0.

This table shows that 58 per cent did not reach Model L, and 79 per cent did not reach Model M in 60 minutes. The total scores reported for each class are therefore largely the result with four models tried, which is a meagre basis for drawing conclusions about relative mechanical ability. The time for 8th grade boys should be extended to, say, 90 minutes, to obtain the benefit of all models.

4. CONCLUSIONS

This series requires more time than is generally practicable in school testing, and apparently does not yield as valuable (per unit of time spent) diagnosis as sets composed of longer series of easier models. It seems doubtful that as good a measure of this type of ability is obtained in 60 minutes with Original Series II as in 30 minutes with Single I or II (developed later). The labor of scoring is also greater in the former.

FIG. 3. Recognition Test.

SECTION VII

RECOGNITION OF MECHANICAL DEVICES OR MECHANICAL INFORMATION TEST

I. GENERAL NATURE

Following out more specifically the idea of identifying mechanical objects and mechanical parts by name, a series of small mechanical objects ranging from the very simplest obtainable to those comparatively technical, e.g., from a common wood screw to the parts of a spark plug, were fastened on an 8 inches by 15 inches stiff cardboard, to fit into a flat cardboard box about $1\frac{1}{4}$ inches high. Fig. 3 gives a general idea of the appearance of this test.

2. LIST OF MECHANICAL DEVICES IN RECOGNITION TEST I

The list of names which follows was given to each person to be tested. The subject was instructed to find the name of each article in the box and to write its identification number opposite the name:

a. Bushing for packing nut of spark plug
b. Cabinet door hook
c. Carriage bolt
d. Catch for cabinet door hook
e. Central insulation for spark plug
f. Center punch
g. Common ten penny nail
h. Common washer
i. Curtain rod fixture
j. Cotter pin
k. Coping-saw blade
l. Cut nail
m. Dowel screw
n. Drive hook
o. Drill
p. Eight penny finishing nail
q. Expansion lug nut
r. Flat head harness rivet
s. Flat head wood screw

t. Fuse wire
u. Gasket or washer for making hose coupling
v. Gimlet
w. Glazier's point for fastening glass
x. Glass cutter
y. Hack saw
z. Hinge
*a*1. Insulating plug for electric light
*b*1. Jam nut or first nut for top of spark plug
*c*1. Lock washer
*d*1. Machine bolt
*e*1. Main body of spark plug
*f*1. Nail set
*g*1. Packing nut for spark plug
*h*1. Patent box or mitre frame fastener
*i*1. Picture nail

21

*j*1. Pipe reducer bushing
*k*1. Plumb bob
*l*1. Roller skate wrench and key
*m*1. Round head rivet
*n*1. Saw screw
*o*1. Shade fixture for nonrevolving end
*p*1. Shelf stop or support
*q*1. Set screw
*r*1. Small hasp
*s*1. Soft solder
*t*1. Staple for small hasp

*u*1. Stove bolt
*v*1. Tar paper cap to prevent paper from tearing
*w*1. Thumb nut
*x*1. Wedge for tool handles
*y*1. Wedge to prevent window from rattling
*z*1. Trunk caster
*a*2. Window sash fastener
*b*2. Window lift
*c*2. Window shade fastener, nonrevolving end

3. RESULTS WITH RECOGNITION TEST

This test was given to 205 pupils of the Forest Park School, Springfield, Mass., in coöperation with Mr. J. L. Riley, then principal, and Mr. W. R. Cole, in charge of industrial arts courses. The pupils had been divided into selected classes as indicated below. The average scores and average deviation of each, obtained in 30 minutes, were as follows:

No.	Grade	Group	Average Score Out of a Possible 55	Average Deviation
40	6B boys	Regular	14.7	5.3
19	7B "	Practical Arts	20.7	7.5
18	7B "	Regular Manual Training	16.4	6.7
17	7B "	Especially Bright	19.8	4.9
22	8B "	Regular Manual Training	20.0	8.0
89	9B and 9A	Boys, Regular	28.0	6.5
60	6B girls	Regular	9.4	5.5

Of these, the Practical Arts group were boys who had elected to take the maximum shop work available, spending much more time in the shop than any other group. The Regular Manual Training group spent much less,—1½ hours per week in the shop, —while the Regular group spent even less, and was composed of undifferentiated pupils.

The Especially Bright class was composed of pupils selected by teachers as able to progress faster than the others, being promoted at shorter intervals.

The average scores for each group given above show that the

task is too difficult for pupils of all these grades. Even the 9th
grade has an average score barely over 50 per cent perfect, while
the others fall much lower. As is to be expected, the Practical
Arts group score slightly higher than the others of same grade.
The grade progression from 6th to 9th appears to be constant,
suggesting that the experience needed to recognize these 55 objects and their names is gradually gained more and more by all as
they become older. Judging from these data the average 9th
grade boy knows about twice as many of these objects and their
names as does the 6th grade boy. The Practical Arts 7B grade
group scores slightly higher than the Regular Manual Training
8B grade,—a gain of one year. Original mechanical interest and
ability, as well as the extra training, no doubt contribute toward
producing this result. The girls' scores show that the test is
entirely too hard for 6B girls.

But only very limited inferences can be drawn from averages of
a single unstandardized test. To obtain checks on these scores
the assembling test, Original Series I, was given to a number of
the same groups. The number who took this test and average
scores were as follows:

No.	Grade	Group	Average Score	Average Deviation
17........	7B	Practical Arts	73.0	7.9
20........	7B	Regular Manual Training	68.9	6.4
17........	7B	Especially Bright	72.8	7.2
21........	7A	Regular Manual Training	65.2	14.9

The Practical Arts group again scored higher than the Regular
Manual Training group of same grade, and were again followed by
the Especially Bright group. This test, however, was found to be
much too easy for these grades. The scores are therefore largely
a comparison of the *speed* with which each pupil could assemble
the models.

4. CORRELATIONS

To obtain a still further check, teachers were asked to rank
their classes in several school subjects. The order of merit in
algebra, geography and literature was combined (tentatively
weighting all equally) into one composite "school subject" rank.

3

From these three measures a number of coefficients of correlation were computed. These are shown in Table VI below. Since each group was unavoidably small, and necessarily ranked by a different teacher, the identity and number in each group is indicated to avoid giving misleading figures.

TABLE VI

COEFFICIENTS OF CORRELATION BETWEEN RECOGNITION TEST, CONSTRUCTION TEST ORIGINAL SERIES I, AND SCHOOL SUBJECT

No. of Boys	Grade	Group	r =
19.........	9B	Recognition and School Rank	.08
20.........	8B	Recognition and School Rank	− .39
17.........	7B	Especially Bright Recognition and School Rank	.02
19.........	7B	Practical Arts Recognition and School Rank	.31
16.........	6B	Regular Recognition and School Rank	.01
20.........	7B	Manual Training (Regular) Recognition and School Rank	.23
16.........	7B	Especially Bright Construction Test and School Rank	.12
16.........	6B	Regular Construction Test and School Rank	.08
19.........	7B	Practical Arts Construction Test and School Rank	− .08
20.........	7B	Manual Training Construction Test and School Rank	.24
20.........	8B	Recognition and Rank in Manual Training	− .31
17.........	7B	Especially Bright Recognition and Construction Scores	.55
16.........	6B	Regular Recognition and Construction Scores	.42
19.........	7B	Practical Arts Recognition and Construction Scores	.22
20.........	7B	Manual Training (Regular) Recognition and Construction Scores	.19
18.........	7A	Practical Arts Recognition and Construction Scores	.49
27.........	6B	Regular Recognition and Construction Scores	.47
21.........	7A	Manual Training (Regular) Recognition and Construction Scores	.71
35.........	6B	Girls Recognition and Construction Scores	.26

The groups being in each case small, the probable error is large, but the agreement between similar group correlations tends to obviate this. While the data are inadequate and the measurements crude, there is evidence that the true correlation between rank in school subjects and the Recognition Test is near zero. Between the Construction Test and school subjects the correlation is also low. Other data not here available indicates that it is not generally over .40. There is, however, some evidence of correlation between the two mechanical tests, but the coefficients are too low to be significant, the average of the coefficients here reported being 41.4. But while it is probable that there are similar elements in the two tests, mere inspection shows that the two tasks are of different character. A boy may assemble a dozen devices without knowing *the technical name* of any of them.

5. RELATIVE "COMMONNESS" OF EACH DEVICE

One other tabulation is of interest, namely, the relative frequency of right answers for each of the 55 devices, or the degree of "commonness" of each.

On the following page is a tabulation of the numbers of right answers for each device—for 57 boys, arranged in order of difficulty.

The results are somewhat surprising in several cases. The hack-saw blade ranks second, while the coping-saw blade ranks forty-second. The roller skate wrench and key is the easiest of all, and the first one on the list, bushing for packing nut of spark plug, is the hardest of all, while the jam nut or first nut for top of spark plug is no more difficult than the window lift. The cotter pin is no more difficult than the glass cutter, and so on.

RELATIVE FREQUENCY OF CORRECT ANSWERS FOR EACH DEVICE IN RECOGNITION TEST ARRANGED IN ORDER OF DIFFICULTY

57 Boys. 7th to 9th Grade

Forest Park School, Springfield, Mass.

Name of Device	Number Correct
l1. Roller skate wrench and key	50
y. Hack-saw blade	48
x. Glass cutter	47
z. Hinge	47

Name of Device	Number Correct
j. Cotter pin	47
v1. Tar paper cap to prevent paper from tearing	46
s. Flat head wood screw	46
h. Common washer	45
k. Curtain rod fixture	44
g. Common ten penny nail	44
b2. Window lift	42
f1. Nail set	42
z1. Trunk caster	41
r. Flat head harness rivet	41
o. Drill	40
m1. Round head rivet	40
p. Eight penny finishing nail	39
i1. Picture nail	36
w. Glazier's point for fastening glass	36
a2. Window sash fastener	34
u. Gasket or washer for making hose coupling	33
c2. Window shade fastener, nonrevolving end	32
1. Cut nail	31
z1. Wedge for tool handles	31
a1. Insulating plug for electric light	29
k1. Plumb bob	29
t. Fuse wire	27
f. Center punch	27
b. Cabinet door hook	27
o1. Shade fixture for nonrevolving end	26
v. Gimlet	24
m. Dowel screw	24
n. Drive hook	23
c1. Lock washer	23
e. Central insulation for spark plug	21
c. Carriage bolt	19
t1. Staple for small hasp	17
e1. Main body of spark plug	17
d. Catch for cabinet door hook	16
b1. Jam nut or first nut for top of spark plug	15
s1. Soft solder	14
w1. Thumb nut	13
k. Coping-saw blade	13
n1. Saw screw	12
q1. Set screw	11
u1. Stove bolt	10
p1. Shelf stop or support	10
d1. Machine bolt	10
r1. Small hasp	9

Name of Device	Number Correct
*h*1. Patent box or mitre frame fastener	9
q. Expansion lug nut	9
*y*1. Wedge to prevent window from rattling	7
*j*1. Pipe reducer bushing	7
*g*1. Packing nut for spark plug	4
a. Bushing for packing nut of spark plug	2

6. CONCLUSIONS

While the results of the Recognition Test are interesting from a research point of view, they are of doubtful value in practical educational testing work.

The experiment was largely to determine the practicability of the method, and while there is no doubt but that there is a certain value in this sort of a test, it has serious limitations, the most important of which is that it does not give promise of measuring general mechanical ability of the kind in which we are most interested, such, e.g., as is measured by the assembling tests. It is purely a test of certain technical information and, moreover, it seems very probable in the light of later results with picture tests that this kind of measure can be obtained with infinitely less labor and expense by the use of pictures,—and these can be increased in range almost infinitely, which is not possible with actual objects. The incidental educational value in the handling of actual mechanical objects, of course, is higher than that in looking at their pictures, and for any purpose, misperceptions will be less frequent. Actual objects also afford a better basis for what may be called mechanical reasoning. But the range of objects is limited. It is extremely difficult to cover a representative field without having at the end an impossible collection of large and heavy objects, impracticable to manage. Its usefulness is therefore largely confined to the laboratory.

SECTION VIII

SINGLE MODEL SERIES

Experience with the Original Assembling Series I and II showed that such sets must be made more convenient and more workable, if possible. It was accordingly decided to attempt the development of a series that would eliminate as many as possible of the faults of the former sets and add possible improvements. The faults were in the main as follows:

The Original Series I was too easy, being adapted only for the lower grades, and was exclusively a copying test. There was no way to insure beginning with the easier models and progressing toward the more difficult ones, as all parts were mixed in one large compartment. Moreover, the boxes were of an awkward shape to handle, and being made of cardboard were not sufficiently strong.

The models of the Original Series II required an average of from 10 to 20 minutes each for most persons. Thus in one hour less than six models could be tried. The element of luck entered into this arrangement, and it is particularly difficult to give just and proper credit for a few partially finished difficult models. The sets were also cumbersome to handle and the models difficult to disassemble. The boxes as designed were about 8 by $4\frac{1}{2}$ by 20 inches.

I. SINGLE SERIES I

After much search and experimentation ten models were selected,—each one simple enough to be solved by an average 7th grade boy in approximately 3 minutes. From the Original Series I those models which had proved most satisfactory were taken, and these supplemented by others, better chosen in the light of past experience. A smaller, narrower, though longer box was next designed,—a group of eight of which when strapped up for carrying are not materially larger or harder to handle than a suit case. In selecting models all that were not "fool proof," easily scorable, and easy to disassemble were rejected. It was also

28

decided to eliminate the extra assembled "copy" model in each
case for the reason that even simple objects would then immediately become sufficiently difficult to constitute a test.
Moreover, it eliminated mere "copying" and introduced what
was believed to be a somewhat "deeper" sampling of the kind of
ability it was desired to measure.   It also cut the cost nearly in
half, made the test only half as heavy, and easier in every way to
manage.   The idea of using the cover as a tray was retained, but
all tools except one small screw driver were eliminated.   These
purely physical features may seem irrelevant and unimportant,
but after a considerable experience with this type of tests it seems
clear that if any such test is not perfected mechanically so that it
is easily workable by any competent examiner,—and is also eco-
nomical of time in scoring,—it defeats its usefulness and is, for
practical purposes, valueless.

The chief improvement hoped for in Single Series I, however,
was increased measuring power, through a wider range of samples,
better control of conditions, and the elimination of copying.   The
reduction of time to 30 minutes, as against 50 to 90 minutes in the
Original Series II was also important since it made it possible to
give the test conveniently within an ordinary school period.

2. MODELS INCLUDED IN SINGLE SERIES I

The models selected were as follows:

A. Ordinary cupboard catch
B. Six links of safety chain
C. Three-piece Hunt paper clip
D. Bicycle bell
E. Wire bottle stopper
F. Clothes pin
G. Shut-off for rubber tubing
H. Push button
I. Small rim lock
J. Mouse trap

The general method of scoring previously adopted was retained,
in which each model perfectly assembled was scored 10 points, and
partial scores assigned each model according to an arbitrary
schedule of values ranging from 1 to 9.

Thirty minutes was found to be sufficient for at least 80 per cent of 6th grade children, and was adapted as standard. A perfect score in 30 minutes was accordingly scored 100 points. In addition a speed bonus of one-half point for each minute under 30 which was not used was added. (This, however, occurs but seldom.) Fig. 4a shows this series in its final form after the models had been scaled.

The instructions which are printed on the cover of each box are as follows:

DO NOT OPEN THIS BOX UNTIL TOLD
TO DO SO

Directions

In this box there are some common mechanical things that have all been taken apart. You are to take the parts and put them together as they ought to be; that is, you are to take the parts and put them together so that each thing will work perfectly.

Do not copy what your neighbor is doing but work absolutely by yourself. Turn the box so that the hinges are towards you. When opeɳed in this position the cover forms a tray in which to work.

Do not break the parts. Everything goes together easily if you do it in the right way. Begin with Model A; then take Model B; then C; and so on. If you come to one that you cannot do in about 3 minutes, go on to the next. The person who gets the most things right gets the highest score.

Preliminary Trials with the Single Model Series. Experience with this series quickly demonstrated it to be an improvement over the earlier ones. The extended range of models, each of which can be solved in a comparatively short interval of time (averaging from 1 to 5 minutes) was found to offer a better chance for mechanical ability to show itself. It afforded a better sampling of a pupil's ability since he had ten chances instead of four or less (as was the case with the Original Series II) in a period of 30 minutes.

The advisability of continuing the "single" model idea, that is, the eliminating of the extra assembled copy model was considered both on the basis of the administrative advantage, and on the basis of the resulting efficiency of the test. In order to test the

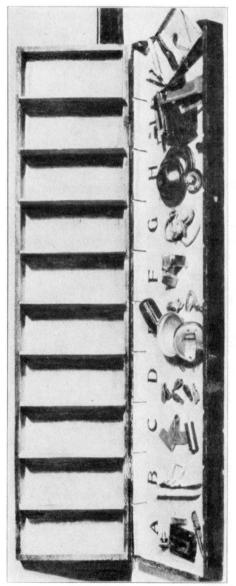

Fig. 4a.　Single Series I.　Final Form.

latter point a group of 62 pupils were given a special test as follows:

From the twenty models later available, ten, which were of such a nature as to lend themselves advantageously to being *disassembled* as well as assembled by the pupils, were made up into a first series, called the "disassembling-assembling criterion set." Here the pupils were first permitted to take apart each model, and, after this operation had been scored and boxes inspected, the pupils were immediately required to assemble the models which they had previously disassembled.

This probably constitutes a more thorough test than either the assembling with, or without a copy model alone, but is of course much more laborious and costly in time. A single series of different models was then given the same pupils, to afford an opportunity for comparison. The correlation between these two tests was estimated from these results to be between .6 and .7, indicating a fairly high correspondence. In order to afford another check, shop teachers' ranks were obtained for the groups included. Fortunately, it was possible to obtain the independent rankings of two such shop teachers, the intercorrelations of which averaged .91, justifying considerable reliance in these ranks as criteria by which to judge a test. The correlations between the shop rank and each of the tests was then computed. Between disassembling-assembling and shop rank, $r = .58 \pm .06$, and between assembling only and shopwork, $r = .61 \pm .06$, indicating that the single series probably is at least equally as good a measure as the disassembling-assembling series. More experimentation should, of course, be carried on to establish more precisely these points, but it was not practicable in this instance. From the administrative standpoint the single model series are in every way advantageous,—unless it be that the opportunity for cheating is somewhat greater. But by ordinary precautions this factor was easily controlled.

On the whole, therefore, it seemed justifiable to continue the further development of the single model series.

3. SINGLE SERIES II

Following out the success with Single Series I, the next task undertaken was accordingly to form a second similar set supposedly about parallel in difficulty with Single Series I.

This was called Single Series II. Here the attempt was again made to select only models which in the light of past experience seemed thoroughly practicable for this purpose. This means they must be sufficiently difficult to present a real problem, and yet be workable. They must be of such a size and nature as to fit conveniently into a series,—must not demand too much mere physical strength, nor special assembling tools, must represent considerable variety, and must correlate fairly well with the same criterion. Particularly only those which can be very quickly disassembled should be included. In the preparation of this series one further step was taken than before in the search for suitable models. Certain stock commercial articles were partially remade in such a way that they can with this modification be disassembled and assembled; for example, a rivet may be replaced by a removable pin without destroying the identity and essential characteristics of the article. A screw may replace a rivet in the same way. This makes available many more models.

As previously pointed out, one of the difficulties met in employing physical objects of this kind as test material, as opposed to printed problems which can be produced at minimum cost, modified *ad infinitum*, and reproduced at will, is that the former are lacking in just these characteristics. Thus, while the models selected seem commonplace when found, the task of finding objects that will meet all requirements is considerable. A troublesome point has been met repeatedly in the fact that articles of this character are continually disappearing from the market, so that it frequently happens, after a model has been standardized, that it is unprocurable except at the exorbitant expense of buying new dies or patterns, for "making it up special." The most practical method of overcoming this circumstance has been to continually standardize new models in terms of old ones, so that a comparatively large number of known difficulty are available. In addition a practice has been made of selecting fairly staple articles. One reason each model must be standardized individually is to afford units or models of known difficulty to be used as substitutes for articles unprocurable after they have been standardized. This introduces difficulties, but cannot well be avoided.

Fig. 4b shows general appearance of Single Series II in its final form.

Fig. 4b. Single Series II. Final Form.

4. MODELS INCLUDED IN SINGLE SERIES II

The list of models as first tried out was as follows:

A. Elbow catch   F. Calipers
B. Rope coupling   G. Rubber stopper
C. Toy pistol   H. Four-piece paper clip
D. Expansion nut   I. Double acting hinge
E. Sash fastener   J. Lock

Preliminary Trial of Single Series II with Single Series I.
Preliminary trials of this series indicated the models all to be
serviceable. Preliminary scaling indicated also that they were of
a slightly better "spread" or distribution as regards relative difficulty. The two series were now given to some 300 pupils and on
the basis of these data the further refinement of the material was
undertaken. As a preliminary it was thought advisable to check
up the question of the contributory value of each new model.

5. CORRELATION OF EACH OF 20 MODELS WITH CRITERION

The criterion here adopted was the total raw score in 20 models.
With this each model was correlated with results as shown below
for 50 thirteen-year-old boys.

FIRST SINGLE SERIES I

A. Cupboard catch	.67	F. Clothes pin	.68
B. Chain	.54	G. Rubber hose	.43
C. Hunt paper clip	.77	H. Push button	.31
D. Bicycle bell	.64	I. Lock No. 1	.48
E. Exp. rubber stopper	.06	J. Wire stopper	.48

FIRST SINGLE SERIES II

A. Elbow catch	.19	F. Calipers	.31
B. Rope coupling	.68	G. Caster	.37
C. Pistol	.73	H. Paper clip No. 4	.68
D. Expansion nut	.64	I. Double hinge	.13
E. Sash fastener	.37	J. Lock No. 2	.48

While it might be theoretically desirable to retain only models
correlating very high with this criterion, the practical consideration of the difficulty of obtaining suitable models made it seem
advisable not to discard any model which had been found to work
well in the series. Moreover, a low correlation with this criterion
is no evidence for assuming a low correlation with other equally
valid criteria.

Section IX

Scaling

As in the case of Series I,[1] arbitrary, partial and perfect score values were assigned in Series II [2] for various degrees of excellence in attempted solutions of each model. Each model correct was counted 10 points, as before. Thus with the models roughly in order of difficulty within each set, and with these partial score values, a working method of scoring each individual was established. But at best this procedure is crude. The difficulty-distances between models are by this method unknown,—that is, the exact difficulty of each model, as compared with any other, is undetermined, and no account is taken of the form of distribution. However, in dealing with this special type of problem a large part of the task consists in the experimentation necessary to discover and perfect models, as well as in the special technique involved in managing them. A series of mechanical objects highly perfected, in so far as finesse in scaling and theoretical treatment is concerned, might still be impracticable and largely useless for actual work. But having previously taken up these points, and having selected material so as to meet these requirements, the next logical step is the refinement of the mathematical technique.

I. A NEW METHOD OF SCALING: THE McCALL METHOD

In the matter of scaling each individual model to determine its relative difficulty, and in the scaling of each series as a whole, a number of methods were possible. The theory of scaling material of this type is not different from verbal material, except for peculiar items such as the short series of problems necessitated by physical limitations. But these are incidental. The literature of test making contains abundant examples of ways of scaling. In fact, it is the variation in methods and technique that is now most disconcerting, for since much of the procedure is arbitrary

---

[1] See sample score sheets in Appendix.

[2] For sake of brevity, and since previous series have been discontinued, the term "Single" series will henceforth be dropped, all series being single unless otherwise specified.

it becomes more and more confusing as each scale comes out, based on some new modification in procedure. Fortunately, at the time of this research a growing movement, fostered by Professors Thorndike, McCall, and others, has developed for the standardization of technique in the scaling process. Even though that standardization be based largely on mutual agreement to adhere to an arbitrary procedure, the important thing is the agreement on some one definite method.

In the interest of uniformity, therefore, as well as on the basis of the advantages incident to it, the McCall method of scaling has been adopted.[1]

Advantages of the Method. As has been suggested, the chief advantage lies in the direction of adopting uniformity of method, making possible direct comparison of final scores for tests of various abilities. Just as a series of Fahrenheit thermometers used respectively for measuring the temperature of one's bath, blood, room, automobile radiator, baby's milk, etc., etc., will record the final results in comparable and meaningful units (which we call "degrees"), just so it should be possible to compare units of any number or variety of mental abilities.

Adopting a uniform procedure involves at least three important items:

1. The agreement as to a basis for scaling, that is, what grade or age should be used in determining scale values.
2. The agreement as to a common unit.
3. The agreement as to a uniform zero point, or point of reference.

Scales have in the past been constructed on the basis of this grade or that, or on the basis of several grades combined. Units have been of all kinds,—the number of right answers, per cent right, probable errors or standard deviations of various grades and ages. Zero points have been located at practically as many different points as there are scales.

Professor McCall's method proposes to standardize these points as follows:

a. The basis of scaling adopted by mutual agreement by a number of investigators is the total distribution of children whose ages range from 12:0 to 13:0 years—no matter in what grades found. The reason for the choice

---

[1] Wm. A. McCall, *How to Measure in Education,* Macmillan Company. Also *Teachers College Record,* March, 1921.

of 12-year-olds in preference to others is that it has been found through researches by Thorndike, Kelley, and others, that with this group a more normal distribution is found than for any other age, since this group is least affected by the factors of school elimination.

 b. The standard unit adopted is one tenth of *1 S.D. of the 12-year-old distribution*, which unit McCall proposes to call "T" in honor of Professors Thorndike and Terman, early advocates of some such standard practice.

 c. The standard point of reference is to be the mean 12-year-old, with the zero point arbitrarily (but apparently reasonably) located at 5 S.D. below the mean. Scale values thus defined will henceforth in this report be referred to as "T-Scale" values.

 d. Each test scaled as a whole. The important departure in this method is that the test is scaled *as a whole.* Each possible "*number right*" *on the whole test*—no matter which elements are included—is given a difficulty value, first in terms of "per cent of 12-year-olds who exceeded plus half those who reached" that partial, and then, to take account of the form of distribution, this percentage is converted into the corresponding S.D. value of 12-year-old by means of a table. Such a table appears on page 44. The two extremes of this table, it will be noted, represent such minute percentages that in practice the ends of the scale are never actually reached. The table will, of course, be recognized as a representation in round numbers of the normal surface of frequency, whose two extremes are infinite, but are here arbitrarily placed at −5 S.D. and +5 S.D. For most scales the table range will lie between, say, 15 to 20 and 75 to 80, and this is a sufficiently large range to provide adequate differentiation.

 McCall has thus adopted the methods employed by Buckingham, Trabue, Woody, and others, for determining the difficulty of each scale element, to the determination of the difficulty of each possible percentage of right answers for the test as a whole. This ignores the relative difficulty of each individual element as stressed by previous scale makers,—except for the general recommendation, advising placing the elements in the general order of difficulty for all grades to be tested, to best insure that the pupil will attempt all the problems which he has any chance of solving. The method takes advantage of the fact that because a given element is most difficult for the greatest per cent of pupils in general, there is no certainty that it will be most difficult for any particular pupil. Some other element may for him be the most difficult.

 The method avoids the more or less precarious and especially laborious procedure of measuring inter-grade distances which is based on assumptions which have never been adequately sustained. It is also much simpler than the former methods, and makes it possible to standardize easily many achievement tests in terms of T-Scale values. It avoids the other laborious and somewhat involved 20–80 per cent method used by Thorndike, in scoring the Alpha Reading test or the 50–50 per cent method used by Kelley in the scoring of the Kelley-Trabue Completion Exercises.

2. RELATIVE DIFFICULTY OF EACH MODEL

The next task would then logically be to determine the T-Scale values of each possible number right for Series I and for Series II. Before doing this, however, it is necessary to examine more closely whether the order in which the models were at first placed in each test is in accordance with their real difficulties. To enable us to observe this point the percentage of correct answers for each model for grades 6, 7 and 8 were computed with their S.D. equivalents. For convenience all the models, that is, both Series I and Series II, were thrown together and all the results tabulated in Table VII. A glance at this table shows at once that the most striking fact is the similarity of difficulties for all of the 20 models, for any given grade, or on the average for all the grades. It means that the 20 models,—selected on the basis of personal estimate as being of a variety of difficulties, are really not very different,—the total range of either series being (on the basis of the average difficulty for the three grades) only about 2 S.D. Fig. 5, showing this fact, also shows that there are "gaps and bunchings" of the models of each series, with Series II a little more difficult on the whole. Theoretically, it is desirable to have a larger range in scale values, but in this case we must keep in mind that there are but ten elements, and to spread ten problems out over a long range of, say, 4 to 6 S.D., results in a very "thin" scale, with great unreliability at any one point of the scale.

There is, therefore, a justification for accepting the series as they are, rather than beginning again and substituting, say, three models much easier and three much harder than any at present included, to produce a larger range of difficulties. Ten scale elements grouped fairly close together tend to eliminate mere "luck" scores, since the opportunity is provided to try more than once, at about the same difficulty. So long as the number of zero or perfect scores for the whole test is negligible or small it is likely that the final score is more reliable when based on such a group of models than it would be in the proposed long and thin scale. While the range of difficulties is short, the ten tasks are by no means identical in difficulty, and less so in their nature. We might actually have a scale of ten elements of identical difficulty and identical nature and yet obtain a measure by considering the speed score. This, of course, is not our purpose here, although account is taken of the speed, and hence the score is partially in terms of it. The differing nature of each model makes it

TABLE VII

PERCENTAGE OF RIGHT SCORES FOR EACH MODEL WITH S.D. EQUIVALENTS
Zero = −5 S.D.   N = Series I: 452, Series II, 459

Model	8th Grade		7th Grade		6th Grade		Aver. S.D. Equiv.
	Per Cent Right	S.D. Equiv.	Per Cent Right	S.D. Equiv.	Per Cent Right	S.D. Equiv.	
Cupboard catch .	665	457	714	443	560	485	462
Chain . , ...	286	557	220	577	203	583	572
Hunt paper clip . .	340	541	300	553	252	567	554
Bicycle bell	243	570	222	577	185	590	579
Expansion rubber stopper	182	591	134	611	147	605	602
Clothes pin	445	514	464	509	318	547	523
Rubber hose	231	574	249	568	133	611	590
Push button	206	582	131	612	096	631	608
Lock No. 1	142	607	114	621	062	654	627
Wire stopper	231	574	168	596	086	637	602
Elbow catch	525	494	562	484	380	531	503
Rope coupling . . .	695	449	592	477	202	583	503
Pistol	61	472	615	471	386	529	491
Expansion nut . .	51	497	562	484	228	574	518
Sash fastener	251	567	266	563	189	588	573
Calipers	128	614	146	605	. . .	632	610
Trap	105	625	115	620	028	690	645
Paper clip No. 4	146	605	115	620	050	665	630
Double hinge	073	646	094	632	027	693	657
Lock No. 2	050	665	023	700	. . .	741	683
Totals	. . .	11,201	. . .	11,323	. . .	12,136	. . .
Average	. . .	560	. . .	566	. . .	607	. . .

particularly hazardous to attempt to say that the mechanical ability of a certain boy is, say, 30 in Series I, because he can assemble the cupboard catch, clothes pin and Hunt paper clip, but not the other models. In Series II he may score 60 because of special experience, and the accidental nature of the particular objects included. It very frequently happens that three difficult (as by this determination) models are solved and many easier ones (as by this determination) are not solved. This, of course, occurs in other scales as well, such as reading scales and language scales, but not so frequently because there is greater uniformity and continuity in the nature of the scale elements. It was partly to provide some statistical method of interpreting such scores that the 20–80 per cent and 50–50 per cent methods previously referred to were devised, and partly to provide a simpler method for ac-

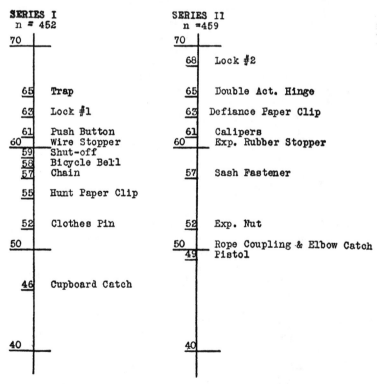

SERIES I
n = 452

70

65 Trap
63 Lock #1
61 Push Button
60 Wire Stopper
59 Shut-off
58 Bicycle Bell
57 Chain
55 Hunt Paper Clip
52 Clothes Pin
50
46 Cupboard Catch

40

SERIES II
n = 459

70

68 Lock #2
65 Double Act. Hinge
63 Defiance Paper Clip
61 Calipers
60 Exp. Rubber Stopper
57 Sash Fastener
52 Exp. Nut
50 Rope Coupling & Elbow Catch
49 Pistol

40

FIG. 5. Scale Difficulty Distribution of Models for Series I and Series II. Av. S.D. Difficulty Values for Each Model for Grades 6, 7 and 8.

4

complishing the same purpose that the McCall method was proposed.

Before going further into this, however, the matter of the order of the models within both series should be settled. Fig. 5 shows that the order of difficulties is not the same as that determined in the beginning by the preliminary trial with a few cases. On the other hand, the differences are not very great.

3. OLD ORDER AND FINAL ORDER OF MODELS

Following is the old order again repeated with the final order for both series:

SERIES I

OLD ORDER	FINAL ORDER
A. Cupboard catch	Cupboard catch
B. Chain	Clothes pin
C. Hunt paper clip	Hunt paper clip
D. Bicycle bell	Chain
E. Wire bottle stopper	Bicycle bell
F. Clothes pin	Shut-off
G. Shut-off	Wire stopper
H. Push button	Push button
I. Lock No. 1	Lock No. 1
J. Trap	Trap

SERIES II

OLD ORDER	FINAL ORDER
A. Elbow catch	Pistol
B. Rope coupling	Elbow catch
C. Pistol	Rope coupling
D. Expansion nut	Expansion nut
E. Sash fastener	Sash fastener
F. Calipers	Expansion rubber stopper
G. Expansion rubber stopper	Calipers
H. Defiance paper clip	Defiance paper clip
I. Double action hinge	Double action hinge
J. Lock No. 2	Lock No. 2

It will be noted that the shift in position is slight in terms of scale distances, as shown in Fig. 5. The question now comes up whether to leave each test as it was originally, in order to preserve its identity, which is desirable in the McCall method of scaling,— or to rearrange the models in terms of the final values obtained. It seemed best to do the latter. Shifting the position of scale elements, however, introduces an error in that the difficulties have a tendency to change when placed in a different position on the scale. But the changes here made are so slight that it is believed no serious change in difficulties will result. In comparing the two scales in Fig. 5, it is clear that the spacing of both the scales would be improved by shifting models from one series to the other, and this could be done since all twenty models were given to the same pupils. But there is an objection to destroying the identity of Series I in that all other records obtained with it then would be lost. The chief body of data collected with this series was that obtained in the Army, where 14,000 cases were tested. This seems sufficiently valuable to justify preserving the identity of Series I, and doing so automatically preserves that of Series II.

4. DIFFICULTIES IN OBTAINING CERTAIN MODELS

In this connection an unfortunate circumstance, illustrating the annoyances incident to working with this type of material, may here be considered. After all the records of the Army experiments were completed for the 14,000 cases, with Single Series I, and the task of scaling and establishing norms for age and grade was taken up, it was discovered that two of the models used in that series were unprocurable because they have been discontinued by the manufacturers. The two articles in question were (1) a small bicycle wrench and (2) a coin safe for holding pennies, nickels and dimes. It was therefore impossible to preserve the exact identity of the series used in the Army, and the only possible alternative was the substitution of other models. Accordingly, this was done. For the bicycle wrench, which was Model A of the Army series, the cupboard catch of our present series was substituted, and for the coin safe, Model E, the wire bottle stopper, as of probably similar difficulties.

These substitutions must therefore be kept in mind when considering the Army series. In order to evaluate them the difficulties were carefully compared. From data in hand the following comparisons were made. For a group of 7th and 8th grades (supplemented by adults, as shown) the difficulty values of the discarded and of the new models were found to be as follows:

OLD (DISCARDED) MODELS

A. *Bicycle Wrench*

No.	Group	Per Cent Right	S.D. Equivalent
95	7th and 8th Grade Boys	.516	
220	Soldiers....................	.525	
	Average.................	.520	.... 50.5

B. *Coin Safe*

95	7th and 8th Grade Boys	.408	
220	Soldiers....................	.440	
	Average.................	.424	.... 49.5
	Average Difficulty of Old Models................		50.0

NEW MODELS

A. *Cupboard Catch*

544	7th and 8th Grade Boys	.689	.450

B. *Wire Bottle Stopper*

544	7th and 8th Grade Boys	.196	.586

Average Difficulty of New Models.............. 51.8
Difference in Difficulty..............18 S.D. or (1.8 T)

Thus it is seen that the average difficulty of the two new models exceeds that of the old discarded ones by .18 S.D., or 1.8 points on the T-Scale. From Army scores obtained with the series, including these two easier models, this amount should be subtracted to make them comparable with the scores herein reported, which were obtained in the final series. This correction is of course only the most probable one. To substitute one model for another without altering the scale values as a whole would require perfect correlation and identical difficulties. All we know here is that the difficulties are reasonably equivalent (we have the estimated differences). The correlation of the four models in question with the total score was found to be for fifty cases as follows:

Wrench with Total Score, 10 models.............$r = .51$
Coin Safe with Total Score, 10 models...........$r = .49$
Cupboard Catch with Total Score, 20 models......$r = .67$
Wire bottle Stopper with Total Score, 20 models ...$r = .48$

5. T-SCALE VALUES FOR EACH RAW SCORE
OF SERIES I AND SERIES II

Having determined the scale difficulties of the elements of these two tests, and having arranged them in what seems to be the best order, we may now consider the matter of scaling each instrument as a whole. This is done by calculating from the distribution of the 12-year-olds the percentages exceeding plus half those reaching each possible raw score value, and then converting these percentages into T-Scale equivalents, in the same way that elements of scales have been treated by other investigators.[1]

The distribution of scores for the two tests as rearranged and scaled is given in Tables IX and X. Because of the small number of cases of 12-year-olds, it was decided to utilize as a check upon them the scores of ages 13, 14 and 15. By computing the distances between the median of the 12-year-olds and that of the 13-year-olds in terms of the percentage of one group which reaches or exceeds the median of the other group, and transmitting this into an S.D. equivalent, and then correcting all of the 13-year-old values by this amount, the 13-year-olds may be utilized as 12-year-olds. This of course assumes a normal distribution for all age-groups thus utilized. Ordinarily it is inadvisable to thus make use of neighboring age-groups, especially those more than one year removed from the 12-year-olds. In this case, however, no marked differences are discernible in the form of distribution for ages 13, 14 and 15, and since the number of cases is small it was thought best to utilize all of the data.

The exact method followed in Tables IX and X is as follows: The S.D. scale values, with −5 S.D. as a zero point, were determined for each age group exactly as for the 12-year-old group. The distances between the 12-year-old group median and the median of each other age group were then calculated by the percentage of overlapping method. Thus the percentage of 13-year-olds who fell below, plus one-half those at the median of the 12-year-olds, was found to be for Series I, . 26. Reference to Table VIII shows the nearest S.D. equivalent in round numbers to be 56.5 S.D. Subtracting this from 50, the midpoint of the 12-year-olds, gives a difference of 6.5 T. That is, the difficulties of attaining each of the various numbers of models right for the 13-

---

[1] Buckingham, Trabue, and others.

year-olds is on the average 6.5 T less than for the 12-year-olds. Similar differences have been computed for each age-group and utilized as a "correction." Adding this correction to the S.D. values of each age group we obtain the 12-year-old equivalents. That is, the older groups are thus utilized as 12-year-olds in order to increase the reliability of our data.   By taking the averages of

TABLE VIII

S.D. Distance of a Given Per Cent Above Zero; Each S.D. Value Is Multiplied by 10 to Eliminate Decimals

The Zero Point Is 5 S.D. Below the Mean

S.D. Value	Per Cent	S.D. Value	Per Cent	S.D. Value	Per Cent	S.D. Value	Per Cent
0.	99.999971	25.	99.38	50.	50.00	75.	0.62
0.5	99.999963	25.5	99.29	50.5	48.01	75.5	0.54
1.	99.999952	26.	99.18	51.	46.02	76.	0.47
1.5	99.999938	26.5	99.06	51.5	44.04	76.5	0.40
2.	99.99992	27.	98.93	52.	42.07	77.	0.35
2.5	99.99990	27.5	98.78	52.5	40.13	77.5	0.30
3.	99.99987	28.	98.61	53.	38.21	78.	0.26
3.5	99.99983	28.5	98.42	53.5	36.32	78.5	0.22
4.	99.99979	29.	98.21	54.	34.46	79.	0.19
4.5	99.99973	29.5	97.98	54.5	32.64	79.5	0.16
5.	99.99966	30.	97.72	55.	30.85	80.	0.13
5.5	99.99957	30.5	97.44	55.5	29.12	80.5	0.11
6.	99.99946	31.	97.13	56.	27.43	81.	0.097
6.5	99.99932	31.5	96.78	56.5	25.78	81.5	0.082
7.	99.99915	32.	96.41	57.	24.20	82.	0.069
7.5	99.9989	32.5	95.99	57.5	22.66	82.5	0.058
8.	99.9987	33.	95.54	58.	21.19	83.	0.048
8.5	99.9983	33.5	95.05	58.5	19.77	83.5	0.040
9.	99.9979	34.	94.52	59.	18.41	84.	0.034
9.5	99.9974	34.5	93.94	59.5	17.11	84.5	0.028
10.	99.9968	35.	93.32	60.	15.87	85.	0.023
10.5	99.9961	35.5	92.65	60.5	14.69	85.5	0.019
11.	99.9952	36.	91.92	61.	13.57	86.	0.016
11.5	99.9941	36.5	91.15	61.5	12.51	86.5	0.013
12.	99.9928	37.	90.32	62.	11.51	87.	0.011
12.5	99.9912	37.5	89.44	62.5	10.56	87.5	0.009
13.	99.989	38.	88.49	63.	9.68	88.	0.007
13.5	99.987	38.5	87.49	63.5	8.85	88.5	0.0059
14.	99.984	39.	86.43	64.	8.08	89.	0.0048
14.5	99.981	39.5	85.31	64.5	7.35	89.5	0.0039
15.	99.977	40.	84.13	65.	6.68	90.	0.0032
15.5	99.972	40.5	82.89	65.5	6.06	90.5	0.0026
16.	99.966	41.	81.59	66.	5.48	91.	0.0021
16.5	99.960	41.5	80.23	66.5	4.95	91.5	0.0017
17.	99.952	42.	78.81	67.	4.46	92.	0.0013
17.5	99.943	42.5	77.34	67.5	4.01	92.5	0.0011
18.	99.931	43.	75.80	68.	3.59	93.	0.0009
18.5	99.918	43.5	74.22	68.5	3.22	93.5	0.0007
19.	99.903	44.	72.57	69.	2.87	94.	0.0005
19.5	99.886	44.5	70.88	69.5	2.56	94.5	0.00043
20.	99.865	45.	69.15	70.	2.28	95.	0.00034
20.5	99.84	45.5	67.36	70.5	2.02	95.5	0.00027
21.	99.81	46.	65.54	71.	1.79	96.	0.00021
21.5	99.78	46.5	63.68	71.5	1.58	96.5	0.00017
22.	99.74	47.	61.79	72.	1.39	97.	0.00013
22.5	99.70	47.5	59.87	72.5	1.22	97.5	0.00010
23.	99.65	48.	57.93	73.	1.07	98.	0.0008
23.5	99.60	48.5	55.96	73.5	0.94	98.5	0.000062
24.	99.53	49.	53.98	74.	0.82	99.	0.000048
24.5	99.46	49.5	51.99	74.5	0.71	99.5	0.000037
....	.....	....	.....	....	.....	100.	0.000029

TABLE IX
ASSEMBLING TEST—SERIES I
T-SCALE SCORES FOR EACH NUMBER RIGHT. WITH PERCENTAGE OF EACH AGE GROUP WHO REACH OR EXCEED EACH SCORE

Total Number of Cases—1,361

No. of Problems Right×10	T-Scale Score	Age 12 Per Cent Exceeding + One-half Reaching	Age 13 Per Cent Exceeding + One-half Reaching	Age 14 Per Cent Exceeding + One-half Reaching	Age 15 Per Cent Exceeding + One-half Reaching	Adult Men (Army) Per Cent Exceeding + One-half Reaching
0 to 1	24	99.6	0	0	00	100
2 to 3	30	98.7	0	99.8	0	99
4 to 5	31	97.3	99.6	96.8	0	99
6 to 7	33	95.1	98.8	95.6	99.5	99
8 to 9	35	91.9	97.6	94.8	99.5	99
10 to 11	38	88.8	94.0	93.6	97.4	98
12 to 13	40	85.2	90.8	91.2	94.1	97
14 to 15	42	81.6	88.7	87.9	91.5	96
16 to 17	43	78.9	85.9	85.1	89.8	95
18 to 19	44	75.3	82.3	82.3	88.2	95
20 to 21	45	71.2	77.9	80.3	86.6	94
22 to 23	46	67.2	77.9	78.3	85.5	93
24 to 25	47	62.2	73.8	75.8	83.4	92
26 to 27	48	58.1	71.4	72.2	81.2	91
28 to 29	49	55.0	69.0	67.8	79.1	90
30 to 31	50	49.6	62.9	65.4	75.9	88
32 to 33	51	43.3	57.7	63.7	71.5	87
34 to 35	52	37.9	54.9	60.6	68.5	87
36 to 37	53	32.9	51.6	56.9	65.6	87
38 to 39	54	28.4	48.0	54.9	63.0	87
40 to 41	55	23.9	45.6	51.6	61.3	78
42 to 43	56	20.8	43.2	46.8	58.1	75
44 to 45	57	18.5	38.7	42.0	54.4	72
46 to 47	58	16.7	33.1	37.9	52.2	69
48 to 49	59	14.5	28.7	35.9	51.1	66
50 to 51	60	11.3	25.4	33.9	47.9	63
52 to 53	60	9.0	22.6	31.1	44.7	60
54 to 55	61	9.0	19.8	29.5	42.0	57
56 to 57	62	7.2	17.1	28.3	42.0	54
58 to 59	62	7.2	16.2	25.4	38.2	51
60 to 61	63	5.4	14.5	22.6	35.0	47
62 to 63	64	5.4	12.9	22.6	31.8	44
64 to 65	64	5.4	11.3	19.0	26.9	41
66 to 67	65	5.1	9.7	19.0	22.6	38
68 to 69	66	4.1	8.5	16.2	20.5	35
70 to 71	67	3.2	7.3	13.7	17.3	31
72 to 73	68	3.2	7.3	11.7	13.5	28
74 to 75	68	3.2	6.1	10.1	10.8	25
76 to 77	69	3.2	6.1	8.5	8.7	22
78 to 79	70	2.3	5.3	5.7	8.7	19
80 to 81	72	1.4	5.3	3.7	6.0	17
82 to 83	74	.4	3.7	2.9	3.8	14
84 to 85	74	....	3.7	2.0	3.8	11
86 to 87	75	....	2.4	1.2	3.8	9
88 to 89	75	....	2.4	1.2	2.2	7
90 to 91	79	....	.8	1.2	.5	6
92 to 93	80	....	.8	.4	....	5
94 to 95	80	....	....	....	....	4
96 to 97	81	....	....	....	....	3
98 to 99	81	....	....	....	....	2
100 to 101	82	....	....	....	....	1
102 to 103	82	....	....	....	....	...
104 to 105	83	....	....	....	....	...
106 to 107	83	....	....	....	....	...
108 to 109	84	....	....	....	....	...
Median T-Score		50	53	56	60	64

TABLE X

ASSEMBLING TEST—SERIES II

T-SCALE SCORES FOR EACH NUMBER RIGHT, WITH PERCENTAGE OF EACH
AGE GROUP WHO REACH OR EXCEED EACH SCORE

Total Number of Cases = 459

No. of Problems Right×10	T-Scale Score	Age 12	Age 13	Age 14	Age 15
		Per Cent Exceeding + One-half Reaching	Per Cent Exceeding + One-half Reaching	Per Cent Exceeding + One-half Reaching	Per Cent Exceeding + One-half Reaching
0 to 1	27	99.6	99.6	0	0
2 to 3	29	98.7	99.6	00	0
4 to 5	32	97.0	98.8	99.6	99.0
6 to 7	35	94.0	97.6	98.8	96.9
8 to 9	37	91.0	97.6	98.0	95.3
10 to 11	39	87.5	94.8	96.4	93.7
12 to 13	41	84.1	91.6	93.6	93.7
14 to 15	42	80.2	91.6	91.2	92.2
16 to 17	44	75.9	89.5	88.3	90.0
18 to 19	45	71.6	86.2	85.1	87.9
20 to 21	46	66.0	85.5	81.5	86.9
22 to 23	47	60.8	83.1	76.6	86.9
24 to 25	48	56.1	78.3	72.6	85.8
26 to 27	49	50.5	74.6	70.2	82.2
28 to 29	50	43.6	73.8	68.2	80.0
30 to 31	51	37.5	71.4	64.9	76.4
32 to 33	52	32.8	67.4	62.5	73.7
34 to 35	54	28.1	62.1	60.9	67.9
36 to 37	55	23.7	56.9	58.1	62.2
38 to 39	55	20.7	53.7	54.9	59.5
40 to 41	56	18.6	50.4	52.9	56.4
42 to 43	57	16.0	47.2	51.6	51.6
44 to 45	58	16.0	43.6	49.2	47.9
46 to 47	58	13.8	39.9	46.8	45.8
48 to 49	59	11.7	35.9	45.6	44.8
50 to 51	60	11.7	31.9	44.0	41.6
52 to 53	61	9.5	29.5	41.6	36.4
54 to 55	61	9.5	25.4	38.7	32.7
56 to 57	62	7.8	21.8	34.3	29.5
58 to 59	63	7.8	20.1	29.9	23.7
60 to 61	64	7.8	17.4	26.6	17.9
62 to 63	65	6.5	13.3	23.0	14.8
64 to 65	66	6.5	10.9	20.2	13.2
66 to 67	67	5.2	8.5	17.4	11.6
68 to 69	68	5.2	6.1	14.1	9.
70 to 71	70	3.9	5.3	11.7	6.9
72 to 73	70	3.9	5.3	9.3	5.8
74 to 75	71	2.2	4.5	7.7	5.8
76 to 77	72	2.2	3.7	6.9	4.8
78 to 79	74	.9	2.0	6.1	4.8
80 to 81	74	....	2.0	4.9	4.8
82 to 83	77	....	.4	2.9	3.2
84 to 85	77	....	....	2.9	1.6
86 to 87	78	....	....	1.2	1.6
88 to 89	78	....	....	1.2	1.6
90 to 91	80	....	....	1.2	.5
92 to 93	81	....	....	.4	....
94 to 95	81	....	....	....	....
96 to 97	82	....	....	....	....
98 to 99	82	....	....	....	....
100 to 101	83	....	....	....	....
102 to 103	83	....	....	....	....
104 to 105	84	....	....	....	....
106 to 107	84	....	....	....	....
108 to 109	84	....	....	....	....
110 to 111	85	....	....	....	....
Median T-Scores		50	56	58	60

N. B.—Tables for Series III not yet available.

ages 12, 13, 14 and 15 as well as the 12 we have a fairly accurate T-Scale score for each raw score value. As more records become available the present values can be confirmed or modified, but for the present (1920) these are the best available.

The Final-Scoring Scheme. We have then in Tables IX and X the final scoring scheme for our two revised single series. For any raw score value, that is, the number of models correct,—we have merely to read the T-Scale score. Thus the raw score of unknown meaning has been transmuted into terms of something fixed and defined, namely the variability of 12-year-old boys. If a boy makes a raw score of 3 right on Series I, we may say by referring to Table IX that he has displayed an amount of ability exceeded by just half of 12-year-old boys in general. His T-Scale score is 50. If the number of models correctly solved is, say, 7.5 his T-Scale score is 68, which means that only .032 per cent of 12-year-olds do better. By referring to Table X the interpretation of any score can be made in the same way for Series II. By referring to the distributions for other ages in the appropriate table we may also note the percentile rank for ages older than 12 years. Thus, for example, Table IX enables us to say that if a boy scores 40 (four right) in Series I his T-Score is 55; and we also see that he is exceeded by 23.9 per cent of 12-year-olds, by 45.6 per cent of 13-year-olds, by 51.6 per cent of 14-year-olds, by 61.3 per cent of 15-year-olds, and by 78 per cent of men in the army. This gives us a well-defined meaning for each score.

The Adult Norms. It will be noted in Table IX that norms in Series I are reported for adult men in Column 7. These were obtained from 909 cases in the Army, where the test was given to over 14,000 cases. The 909 cases referred to were all members of a 303d Company of Engineers. As explained on page 59, Series I as used in the Army was 1.8 T less difficult than the present series, and this correction should be kept in mind when making comparisons. For practical purposes, however, Series I as used in the Army and in its present form may be considered identical.

On the basis of the 909 men of the 303rd Engineers the following army norms were compiled, which are for reference included here:

ARMY SERIES

Score (number models right times 10)	Percentile Rank
0	0
10	1.5
20	6.0
30	12.0
40	22.0
50	37.0
60	53.0
70	69.0
80	83.0
90	94.0
98	100.0

These percentile ratings were for convenience apportioned among five letter grades as follows:

Letter Rating	Score Per Cent
A	96–100
B	80–95
C	40–79
D	20–39
E	0–19

Grade Norms. Grade norms are of doubtful significance because of the unscientific manner in which most grading is done, and also because of the special trait we are considering. The overlapping is tremendous, and the differences between grades are small, approximating zero in Grades 7 and 8. Grade means as found are, however, here reported for whatever value they may have:

SERIES I

	Grade 4	Grade 5	Grade 6	Grade 7	Grade 8	H. S.	Adult Men
Mean raw score ..	19	..	37	45	47	50	58
No. of cases	16	..	69	335	274	60	909

SERIES II

	Grade 6	Grade 7	Grade 8
Mean raw score...............	34	41	439
No. of cases..................	71	217	245

Girls' Records. The test has been confined largely to boys, but a few records for girls are available for Series I. These are as follows:

No.	Grade	Mean Raw Score	Mean T-Score	M. D. from Mean Raw Score
96........	Sixth grade	22.9	45.5	12.0
67........	Eighth grade	30.0	50.0	15.5
13........	Teacher Training School students	39.0	54.0	13.7
44........	Graduate students— adult women	45.9	56.5	....

SECTION X

FORM OF DISTRIBUTION OF MECHANICAL ABILITY

In order to convey an idea of the form of distribution for each series for Grades 6, 7, and 8, the following figures are included:

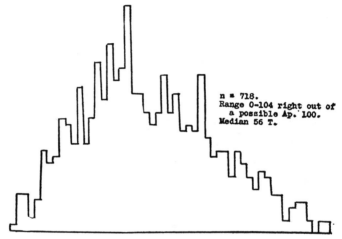

n = 718.
Range 0-104 right out of a possible Ap. 100.
Median 56 T.

FIG. 6.   Series I.   Form of Distribution for Grades 6, 7 and 8 Combined.

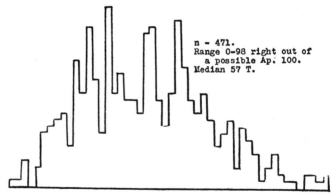

n = 471.
Range 0-98 right out of a possible Ap. 100.
Median 57 T.

FIG. 7.   Series II.   Form of Distribution for Grades 7 and 8 Combined.

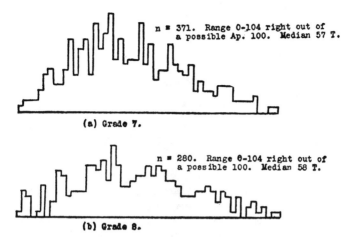

n = 371. Range 0-104 right out of a possible Ap. 100. Median 57 T.

(a) Grade 7.

n = 280. Range 0-104 right out of a possible 100. Median 58 T.

(b) Grade 8.

FIG. 8. Series I. Form of Distribution for Grades 7 and 8.

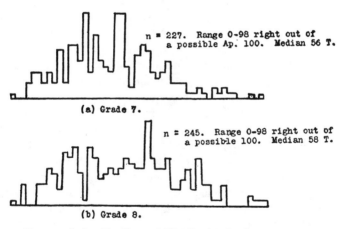

n = 227. Range 0-98 right out of a possible Ap. 100. Median 56 T.

(a) Grade 7.

n = 245. Range 0-98 right out of a possible 100. Median 58 T.

(b) Grade 8.

FIG. 9. Series II. Form of Distribution for Grades 7 and 8.

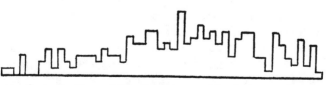

FIG. 10. Series I. Form of Distribution. 200 Men in Army. Range 0-110 Right. Median 64 T.

The Partial Score Factor

Thus far our tests have been given raw scores by the method originally adopted, namely by arbitrarily allowing 10 points for each model assembled perfectly, and partial values of 1, 2, 3, 4, 5, 6, 7, 8, or 9, for various degrees of achievement with each model, as indicated in the score sheets, samples of which are shown in the Appendix. By adding the various partial score values to form the total raw score the range extends from 0 to 100, with a time bonus of one-half point per minute for each minute less than the standard 30 minutes, as explained in the Appendix. A score may occasionally go slightly higher than 100. This provision of relatively fine gradation of raw scores seemed necessary in view of the fact that only ten models can on the average be successfully given in an ordinary school period. The time found most practicable for these tests is 30 minutes, since considerable time is consumed in the handling of the boxes before and after the test.

The Short Form Test. But partial scores are always troublesome and should be eliminated or minimized whenever possible. The question then arises: Can we eliminate partial scores in such a test as this and still preserve most of its efficiency? If so, it would greatly simplify and expedite its use, for much of the time consumed in scoring is given to determining partial values.

To answer this question it is necessary to know the relation between distributions of scores obtained by the regular partial score method and the method of counting "rights only." This is shown by the coefficients of correlation of Table XI. These were obtained in a preliminary study by the "percentage of unlike-signed pairs method" and hence are probably too high.

But if corrected they are still very high. In view of this it is justifiable for certain purposes to score the tests on this basis.

This method of regarding only the perfect scores may appropriately be called the "Short Form Method" and should be so specified whenever used.

For an approximate classification of children into groups with marked average and below average ability this method is reasonably satisfactory,—just how satisfactory may be inferred from the correlations of Table XI.

TABLE XI

CORRELATION BETWEEN SCORES WHEN COUNTING ONLY THOSE MODELS PERFECTLY ASSEMBLED, AND WHEN COUNTING ALL PARTIAL SCORE VALUES IN ADDITION TO THE PERFECT ONES

No.	Series	Grade	$r =$
40	I	8B³	.92
23	I	8B¹	.988
40	II	8B³	.100
38	II	8B³	.995
33	II	8A¹	.995
37	II	6B¹	.988
37	I	7B²	.100
26	II	7B²	.100
40	I	6B³	.976
36	I	7B¹	.94
31	II	5A¹	.100
35	II	4B¹	.826

A more practicable procedure is to give both Series I and II in this short form and to take the average T-Scale scores as final. This allows the pupil twenty models, and an hour of time in which to demonstrate his ability. This method has an advantage in that greater accuracy of scoring results in any test when avoiding the giving of partial scores. In this method in particular reliable boys may quickly be trained to do most of the work of scoring as has previously suggested and as explained in the Appendix, page 93.

Section XII

Series III, Assembling Test, for Lower Grades

In order to provide for younger children than can be tested with Series I and II, a third series was designed to take the place of the original Series I, described in Section III, which, as has been pointed out, had certain defects, but had the advantage of being applicable to grades as low as the third. Experiment with Series III have been begun, and it will be scaled exactly as in the case of Series I and II. The general appearance of first models tried is shown in Fig. 11.

MODELS INCLUDED IN SERIES III

The models of Series III for Grades 3, 4, 5 and 6 were:

A. Bolt and wing nut	F. Key and ring
B. Plain hinge	G. Drawer pull
C. Plain push button	H. Nail clipper
D. Swivel	I. Heavy caster
E. Trunk caster	J. Dater

These models must be considered as tentative only and may be changed after more extensive experimentation. In fact, an improved double series similar to Original Series I (see page 5) would undoubtedly be preferable for these lower grades.

FIG. 11.   Series III.   For Grades 3, 4, 5 and 6.

SECTION XIII

SUPPLEMENTARY MODELS

In the experiments conducted to find suitable models a number were tried out which for various reasons were not included in the final Series I, II and III. There were, beside the thirty models in these series, these models:

31. A long finger-shaped paper clip
32. The roller from a Ford timer
33. A spring hinge
34. A coin safe or holder, for holding nickels, dimes and pennies
35. A small bicycle wrench

These were tried out for a limited number of cases, ranging between 50 and 100. The difficulty values were, however, estimated from the data in hand and were found to be as follows:

TABLE XII

GENERAL SCALE VALUES IN TERMS OF S.D. FOR GRADES 6, 7, AND 8.
S.D. VALUES TRANSMUTED INTO LIKE-SIGNED EQUIVALENTS
WITH 5 S.D. AS ZERO

$n = about\ 50$

	8th Grade		7th Grade		6th Grade	
	Per Cent Right	S.D.	Per Cent Right	S.D.	Per Cent Right	S.D.
31. Finger clip....	.105	.625	0	0	.075	.644
32. Ford timer roller.........	.105	.625	.068	.649	0	0
33. Spring hinge ..	.158	.60	.13	.63	.025	.696
34. Coin safe.....	.47	.508	....	....	....	....
35. Wrench	.842	.40	....	....	....	....

5

Some of these models were discarded for the reason that they are at the time improcurable. This was the case, as has been explained, with models No. 34 and No. 35. Of the other models some were found to involve too much mere physical strength, as in the case of the "finger" paper clip and spring hinge.

SECTION XIV

RELIABILITY

The self-correlation of a test is commonly utilized as a measure of its reliability. If the reliability of a test were perfect, any number of measurements of the same individuals taken with that test would yield precisely the same results. This never is the case with any measuring instrument yet devised. The reliability of various tests, however, varies greatly, and in order to interpret intelligently correlations obtained with a given test the reliability, or self-correlation, must be known. The self-correlation coefficients obtained for these tests are as follows:

Considering Series I and Series II, scored in the regular way (counting partial scores) for 369 cases, 7th and 8th grades, $r = .59 \pm .02$. For 23 graduate university students, men and women, r between Series I and Series II = .75.

For Series I alone, alternate models were correlated as follows: Models A-C-E and B-D-F were each considered as a test,—that is, the two halves of the test were intercorrelated. The coefficients found are:

216 cases, men in Army..........................	$r = .68$
30 cases, 1st year high school boys...............	$r = .80$
116 cases, 7th and 8th grade boys.................	$r = .75$
24 cases, 8th grade girls.........................	$r = .79$
52 cases, 6th grade girls.........................	$r = .06$
60 cases, 6th grade boys.........................	$r = .45$

It is probable from the above coefficients that the true reliability is between .6 and .7. For two groups, the high school class and 7th and 8th grade boys, it runs up even higher. This degree of reliability is probably as high as can generally be obtained with such material, but it is not all that could be desired. It is to be hoped that further experimentation will result in scales of higher reliability.

Section XV

Correlations

The correlations of most interest are those with general intelligence and with other available criteria of mechanical ability.

I. CORRELATIONS WITH GENERAL INTELLIGENCE

The most reliable of the former were obtained from the Army records, which between Army Alpha intelligence test and Series I are as follows:

Camp Taylor, 109 unselected men...................... $r = .323$
Camp Devens, 107, foreign eliminated, but largely inferior
    cases... $r = .35$
Camp Lee, 76 unselected men........................ $r = .30$
Camp Lee, 30 men below 50 in Army.................. $r = .00$ approx.
Camp Lee, 216 men low grade, individually examined..... $r = .00$ approx.
Camp Dix, 909 men, 303d Engineers, unselected......... $r = .51$
Massachusetts School Feeble Minded, 30 cases, with mental
    age... $r = .32$
Same group with officers' ratings..................... $r = .25$
For 100 7th and 8th grade boys, New York Public schools,
    between Series I and composite intelligence score, made up
    of Haggerty, National 1 and 2, Otis, Kelley-Trabue, and
    Meyers... $r = .397$
For same group, same tests, with Series II.............. $r = .338$

2. CORRELATIONS WITH OTHER CRITERIA OF GENERAL MECHANICAL ABILITY

The best available criteria of general mechanical ability of the kind supposedly measured by these tests has been manual training and science teachers' ranks. It frequently is true, however, that these ranks are too unreliable to be trustworthy, because the pupils' abilities are not well known to these shop instructors. An effort has therefore been made to obtain classes having two shop teachers, making it possible to intercorrelate the two rankings for reliability, before considering either of them as a criterion. The coefficients obtained are as follows:

58

Shop Teacher Rank and Series I

27, 7th and 8th grade boys in Lincoln School.................... $r = .83$

15, 8th grade boys in New York City public schools............. $r = .80$

24, 8th grade boys in New York City public schools............. $r = .42$

14, 6th and 7th grade boys, Horace Mann School................ $r = .81$

18, 6th grade boys in Horace Mann School..................... $r = .90$

17, 6th grade boys in Horace Mann School..................... $r = .88$

Section XVI

Summary of Assembling Tests

We have then as a result of our experiments three instruments for measuring mechanical ability of the kind herein described. Two of these, Series I and Series II, are of practically equal difficulty and can be used interchangeably for Grades 5, 6, 7, 8, high school and adults, generally. Series III is much easier, being adapted to Grades 3, 4, 5 and 6.

The norms given are admittedly based on a relatively small number of cases, but because of the method of scaling adopted these can be quickly and continuously substantiated or revised as more records become available. The correlations show that the reliability of any one of the tests is reasonably high as compared with other tests. More than one series now being available, this can be increased by retesting.

The advantages in the method adopted in scaling are chiefly that scores are reported in well-defined terms—namely the variability of 12-year-old boys—and that the scores are directly comparable with T-Scale scores of other tests, as well. The short form of scoring permits the rapid testing of large numbers. As to what the test measures our correlations show that it selects ability markedly different from that discovered by verbal tests of general intelligence,—the correlations never ranging over .5, and for most groups being nearer .4. On the other hand, it does detect those qualities that cause a pupil to excel in the opinion of manual training and science teachers. Whatever this ability is, it is not, however, trade skill, any more than it is verbal intelligence. It is rather a composite of common sense and skill in managing physical objects of a mechanical nature. It might be called general mechanical intelligence and ability. The origin of this ability is not here considered, but its distribution is shown to be largely regardless of ordinary school classification.

Ordinarily we are most interested in determining whether a pupil is unusual in this type of ability, and this the tests show us admirably. As for making hairbreadth distinctions between pupils because of slight differences in scores in these tests, caution must continually be counselled here, as well as in the use of other mental tests.

We have in these tests, then, instruments for obtaining a definite measure of a trait which is generally estimated with great inaccuracy by school authorities as well as by parents and pupils themselves. The shortcomings of the tests have been repeatedly noted in this report. Their advantages and the uses which can be made of them are obvious.

MEASURING MECHANICAL APTITUDE BY MEANS OF ILLUSTRATIONS:
PICTURE TESTS OF MECHANICAL APTITUDE [1]

I. AIM AND PURPOSE

The natural limitation in any "material test," i.e., one requiring physical apparatus, is of course that such tests are somewhat difficult to administer in large school systems where thousands of individuals are to be tested. This is chiefly because the scoring must be done after testing each class before the material can again be used. While a large number of outfits may be available, it is out of the question to have a set for each pupil as with paper tests, and it is therefore not possible to test large numbers in a short time, as can be done with paper tests. Moreover, physical apparatus, while of far more intrinsic interest to the pupils, is of course more cumbersome to handle than mere sheets of paper, and requires somewhat more mechanical skill in scoring and managing.

To meet this increasing need for some means whereby a teacher or principal may quickly obtain some measure of the mechanical abilities of large numbers of pupils in great school systems such as, for example, in New York City, and in survey work generally, the writer set out to develop a series of paper tests of general mechanical aptitude, and to evaluate these in terms of mechanical ability as shown by the assembling tests; by shop ability as shown by rank given by teachers of manual training, and in terms of general intelligence.

These tests involve judgments of mechanical relationships and a general knowledge of things mechanical,—their principles, operation and use. While the actual trial at manipulating devices, such as in assembling tests, is sacrificed, many of the same general mental processes are called for. Because of the difficulty

---

[1] For samples see Stenquist Mechanical Aptitude Tests, published by World Book Co., Yonkers, N. Y.

in obtaining suitable models for assembling tests, they are limited in range, but the moment the problem is transferred to paper an enormously larger range of applications is opened up. Thus, while it is impracticable to use the assembling of a lathe or engine as a test, it is quite as easy to treat such devices by means of pictures and questions as is a paper clip or mouse trap.

If a paper test of mechanical aptitude, even partially as effective as the actual manipulative tests, could be invented to measure the same general trait, it was thought to be quite worth while because of the ease with which it can be utilized for large numbers. The need for something of this kind is particularly urgent in connection with vocational and educational guidance.

Here, as in the assembling tests, the aim is to measure individual differences in that certain general "mechanical bent" or "turn of mind" of children of school age,—well recognized by all, though but vaguely defined in the minds of most persons. The marked distinction between pupils in this kind of ability is, however, well known to every parent, and to every teacher,—particularly to teachers of any form of shop-work: but unfortunately, almost nothing has been done to obtain an exact measure of it. But this ability must not be confused with trade skill, or trade knowledge. The Army trade tests are better adapted to select skilled mechanics. This, however, is not the problem with boys of the upper grades and high school. The problem there is to discover differences in *general* mechanical interests and abilities which will constitute reasonably intelligent bases for guidance.

2. DESCRIPTION

The technical names and language involved in mere verbal questions on mechanics,—including descriptions of mechanical devices and processes, defeat their usefulness as tests of general mechanical ability. Advantage was therefore taken of what is probably the best substitute for objects to actually handle— namely, illustrations of such objects. By means of these it is possible to present a great number of mechanical problems with the utmost ease, without the use of any language, and in addition, a large number of problems in non-technical language by simple questions referring to illustrations.

The method of arranging the illustrations in such a way as to call for a judgment of *relationship* between two or more ideas has previously been employed with marked success by psychologists in verbal and picture tests of general intelligence and other traits. By this method it is often possible with pictures to present a more pertinent and telling question than by technical, verbal description,—and always more easily. The comparison of the mental processes involved in actually manipulating parts of mechanical devices, with those involved in answering the questions presented by the illustration tests, is best portrayed by the correlations shown in actual trial. This is treated statistically in a following section.

Selection of Subject Matter. No test can do more than sample the almost endless variety of mechanical contrivances of man. In complexity, they range from the absurdly simple to the almost infinitely complex—from the stone axe of primitive man to a Mergenthal linotype, or a modern battleship. But generally speaking a few principles and laws of mechanics govern them all, and each new invention is for the most part but a novel combination of old principles for new purposes.

The specific devices selected to be used as the basis of test questions may not therefore be of as great importance as seems apparent at first thought. In these tests a consistent effort has been made to select on the following bases:

1. Devices must be of general interest, and not pertain to very highly specialized trades. Common household articles that are of a mechanical nature are most apt to fall within the experience of every one.

2. The question involved must be as mechanical as possible in its nature, involving a knowledge of, familiarity with, or understanding of the purpose, use, operation, construction, or reason for special size, shape, weight, material, etc., of the device in question.

In the main the models chosen in these tests are common rather than highly specialized devices. No trade or occupation is singled out. But in cases where a somewhat special tool or device *is* included the question asked is of a general mechanical nature, that does not necessarily require acquaintance with that particular device.

While the present series are of a generalized nature, it is clear that a large number of series, each of which, while not strictly a trade test, would nevertheless deal with a restricted field, would be of great value. Thus, for example, there is need for a standardized test of carpentry, cabinetmaking, cement construction, blacksmithing, sheet metal working, etc., particularly in connection with vocational education.

The answering of the questions of these tests involves a certain type of information and ability in perceiving and judging mechanical objects and their characteristics that seems almost instinctive in some individuals, and almost wholly absent in others. But what the psychological processes and principles involved are, is not within the province of this study to attempt to demonstrate. It may not, however, be out of place to point out that the mental thresholds between the type of mechanical ability herein treated— and other skills and information, particularly general intelligence and common sense—are not sharp, clear-cut lines. On the contrary, these abilities probably merge imperceptibly into each other.

Scoring: An Improved Method. Brief mention may be made of the method of scoring, which has been so simplified that it can be done efficiently at high speed by clerical help. In addition to employing the "key" method, a further expedient has been introduced in binding the pages with overlapping margins.[1] By placing all the answers at the edge of the page they are exposed without the necessity of opening each page and repeatedly readjusting the stencil, which, though simple, is wasteful of time. Thus, while as much as five minutes is sometimes required in scoring such a booklet by the old method of opening each page and adjusting the stencil key each time to scattered answers,—by this method it can easily be reduced to from one to two minutes per booklet. Keys are so designed that only one adjustment is necessary.

Ease of scoring, while always subordinate in importance to reliability and efficiency of the measuring power of a test, becomes of great importance to the practical administrator of tests, and, in fact, in large school systems it becomes almost the *sine qua non* of a usable test. For, if scorable only by experts and at great expenditure of time, a test is practically worthless to school administrators who face the alternative of "putting it over" through the machinery at hand,—the teaching and supervisory staff, or else foregoing it altogether.

---

[1] Excluded in first edition.

3. PICTURE TESTS I AND II OF MECHANICAL INFORMATION AND
APTITUDE

A total of 173 questions, some expressed in terms of pictures to
be compared one with another, and some in terms of printed
queries referring to lettered pictures of machines and common
mechanical articles were originally compiled into two tests, I and
II. In Test I was placed only non-verbal material. In Test I
the task is to determine which of five pictures "belongs with, is a
part of, or is used with" each of five other pictures. The total
test has nineteen distinct group elements. The test is scored by
counting the total number of items right.

Test 2 is divided into ten parts, each consisting of from five
to seventeen questions. The first of these consists of nineteen
pictures of mechanical toys, and each of these pictures has been
cut into two parts. The task is then to find the missing part for
each picture. Parts 2, 3, 4 and 5 consist of a series of questions
relating to the mechanical properties of each of four lettered
pictures of typical machines: An ordinary electric bell, a
blower, a countershaft, a power drill press. The questions
asked are, however, answerable by competent persons, even
though they have not had direct experience with these particular machines, as they involve chiefly mechanical reasoning
and perception.

The last group of questions pertains to the construction and
operation of two ordinary derricks. Here as in the other groups
the ability to answer the questions does not depend so much upon
a direct experience with such machines as upon insight into
mechanical principles and usages.

Scale Difficulty Values. After a few preliminary trials had
showed that these tests correlated well with shop teachers' ranks
and with the assembling tests, 664 of Test I and 1087 of Test II
were given to Grades 6, 7, 8 and high school. On the basis of
these records the average relative difficulty of each element was
computed. The results appear as Table XIII for Test I and
Table XIV for Test II.

T-Scale Values for Each Raw Score. The same method of
scaling as employed in the assembling tests has been adopted for
these tests. Tables XV and XVI give the T-Scale values for
each number right for each test. These tables also give the age

distributions for other ages than the 12-year-olds, so that the percentage of any age which exceeds a given score can be seen at a glance. This is the same arrangement as in the case of the assembling tests.

TABLE XIII

PICTURE TEST I*

PERCENTAGE OF RIGHT ANSWERS TO EACH PROBLEM AND S.D. EQUIVALENTS

To Eliminate Minus Signs Zero Is Considered as at −5 S.D.

Problem No.	Grade 6		Grade 7		Grade 8		Average S.D. Equivalent
	Per Cent Right	S.D.	Per Cent Right	S.D.	Per Cent Right	S.D.	
1	.621	47.	.586	48.	.675	45.5	46.8
2	.307	55.	.235	57.	.329	54.5	55.5
3	.321	54.5	.288	55.5	.389	53.	54.3
4	.70	44.5	.534	49.	.618	47.	46.8
5	.679	45.5	.772	42.5	.811	41.	43.0
6	.362	53.5	.316	55.	.314	55.	54.5
7	.562	48.5	.502	50.	.50	50.	49.5
8	.452	51.	.512	49.5	.508	50.	50.2
9	.30	55.	.274	56.	.297	55.5	55.5
10	.262	56.5	.214	58.	.222	57.5	57.3
11	.286	56.	.260	56.5	.232	57.5	56.6
12	.421	52.	.386	53.	.472	51.	52.0
13	.242	57.	.379	53.5	.354	54.	54.8
14	.252	56.5	.309	55.	.372	53.5	55.0
15	.318	55.	.393	53.	.393	53.	53.6
16	.204	58.	.246	57.	.314	55.	56.6
17	.238	57.	.298	55.5	.336	54.5	55.6
18	.142	60.5	.221	57.5	.193	58.5	58.8
19	.128	61.5	.214	58.	.229	57.5	59.0

* One group of ten pictures to be matched is considered one problem.

TABLE XIV
PICTURE TEST II
PERCENTAGE OF RIGHT ANSWERS TO EACH PROBLEM, AND S.D. EQUIVALENTS
To Eliminate Minus Signs Zero Is Considered as at − 5 S.D.

EXERCISE 1

Problem	Grade 5 n = 168		Grade 6 n = 314		Grade 7 n = 228		Grade 8 n = 348	
	Per Cent	S.D.	Per Cent	S.D.	Per Cent	S.D.	Per Cent	S.D.
3	.215	443	.742	435	.885	380	.880	382
4	.57	482	.682	453	.837	402	.772	425
5	.44	515	.534	491	.610	472	.600	474
6	.358	521	.433	527	.470	508	.511	495
7	.53	499	.622	469	.767	427	.765	428
8	.328	545	.423	519	.500	500	.558	485
9	.590	477	.623	469	.790	419	.760	429
10	.405	524	.459	511	.482	505	.495	501
11	.547	488	.602	474	.710	444	.799	416
12	.505	499	.604	473	.759	430	.782	422
13	.62	469	.741	435	.825	407	.852	395
14	.57	482	.642	463	.745	434	.772	425
15	.46	510	.591	477	.695	448	.719	442
16	.50	500	.710	444	.729	439	.747	433
17	.56	485	.699	448	.736	437	.750	432
18	.40	526	.470	501	.535	474	.578	480
19	.815	410	.853	395	.940	344	.917	361

Average: 64 per cent right

EXERCISE 2
Figure 1

1	.388	528	.461	510	.570	480	.735	437
2	.098	629	.121	617	.232	573	.354	537
3	.490	509	.572	412	.769	426	.802	415
4	.047	668	.092	639	.127	614	.189	588
5	.316	548	.484	504	.543	480	.705	446
6	.167	597	.268	562	.399	526	.445	514
7	.035	682	.115	620	.132	612	.216	579
8	.057	658	.086	637	.158	600	.233	573

Average: 37 per cent right
Figure 2

1	.442	520	.423	519	.570	482	.625	468
2	.334	543	.366	534	.519	495	.525	494
3	.238	571	.379	531	.430	518	.605	473
4	.202	583	.283	558	.399	526	.495	501
5	.411	522	.398	526	.456	511	.477	506
6	.173	594	.234	573	.386	529	.460	510
7	.202	583	.229	574	.237	572	.394	527

Average: 42 per cent right
Figure 3

1	.405	524	.553	486	.698	448	.765	428
2	.220	577	.321	546	.390	528	.422	520
3	.460	511	.465	509	.580	480	.564	484
4	.161	599	.252	567	.329	544	.435	514
5	.185	590	.321	546	.232	573	.216	579

Average: 44 per cent right

TABLE XIV—(Cont'd)

EXERCISE 2—(Cont'd)

Figure 4

Problem	Grade 5 n = 168		Grade 6 n = 314		Grade 7 n = 228		Grade 8 n = 348	
	Per Cent	S.D.	Per Cent	S.D.	Per Cent	S.D.	Per Cent	S.D.
1	.430	518	.640	464	.830	404	.875	385
2	.280	559	.321	546	.482	505	.511	497
3	.107	624	.143	598	.280	558	.314	548
4	.053	662	.127	614	.236	572	.330	544
5	.047	668	.137	610	.149	604	.161	599
6	.035	682	.044	671	.127	614	.181	591
7	.214	579	.277	559	.496	501	.482	505
8	.202	584	.204	583	.390	528	.322	546
9	.077	643	.140	608	.241	570	.293	505
10	.340	541	.360	536	.456	511	.451	512
11	.088	635	.146	605	.219	578	.175	593
12	.101	628	.175	594	.202	584	.187	589

Average: 31 per cent right

EXERCISE 3

Section A

	Per Cent	S.D.	Per Cent	S.D.	Per Cent	S.D.	Per Cent	S.D.
3	.452	512	.547	488	.629	467	.652	461
4	.256	566	.277	559	.500	500	.517	496
5	.179	592	.158	600	.324	546	.362	535
6	.316	548	.286	557	.447	514	.457	511
7	.256	566	.261	564	.394	527	.402	525
8	.244	570	.251	567	.486	504	.394	527
9	.244	570	.267	562	.415	521	.385	529
10	.262	564	.242	570	.517	496	.497	501
11	.208	581	.204	593	.405	524	.437	516
12	.280	555	.236	572	.495	501	.500	500
13	.328	545	.236	572	.552	487	.535	491

Average: 38 per cent right

Section B

	Per Cent	S.D.	Per Cent	S.D.	Per Cent	S.D.	Per Cent	S.D.
1	.274	560	.341	541	.517	496	.569	483
2	.328	545	.353	538	.430	518	.434	516
3	.041	674	.124	616	.184	590	.218	578
4	.119	618	.242	570	.258	565	.322	546
5	.234	570	.302	552	.469	508	.506	498

Average: 35 per cent right

Section C

	Per Cent	S.D.	Per Cent	S.D.	Per Cent	S.D.	Per Cent	S.D.
1	.131	612	.219	578	.302	552	.304	551
2	.185	590	.216	579	.280	559	.253	566
3	.226	545	.207	582	.294	554	.282	558
4	.220	578	.232	573	.368	534	.330	544
5	.071	647	.168	596	.268	562	.290	556
6	.244	570	.312	549	.500	500	.422	520
7	.202	584	.242	570	.507	496	.442	575

Average: 31 per cent right

Section D

	Per Cent	S.D.	Per Cent	S.D.	Per Cent	S.D.	Per Cent	S.D.
1	.041	674	.051	664	.224	576	.212	580
2	....	...	.006	751	.013	723	.023	700
3	....	...	....	...	.021	704	.005	758
4	.131	612	.229	514	.334	743	.328	545
5	.119	618	.222	577	.461	510	.391	527

Average: 17 per cent right

TABLE XV.   Showing the Raw Scores (Number Right), T-Score Equivalents, and the Percentile Ranks for Each Age Corresponding Each Score for Test I

Total Number Cases, 1130

Raw Score (Number Right)	T-Score Equivalent	Percentile Rank for each of five ages				
		11 yrs. 6 mos.	12 yrs. 6 mos.	13 yrs. 6 mos.	14 yrs. 6 mos.	15 yrs. 6 mos.
1	15					
2	16					
3	17					
4	18	1				
5	19	1	1			
6	20	1	1			
7	21	2	1			
8	22	2	1			
9	23	2	2			
10	24	3	2	1		
11	25	3	2	1		
12	26	4	3	1		
13	27	4	3	2	1	
14	28	5	3	2	1	
15	29	6	4	3	2	1
16	30	7	4	3	2	1
17	31	8	5	3	3	2
18	32	9	5	4	3	2
19	33	10	6	5	4	3
20	34	11	7	6	5	4
21	35	13	8	7	6	5
22	36	15	10	8	7	6
23	37	17	12	9	8	7
24	38	19	14	10	9	8
25	39	22	16	12	11	9
26	40	25	17	14	12	10
27	41	28	19	16	14	11
28	42	32	21	18	16	13
29	43	36	24	20	18	15
30	44	40	27	23	20	17
31	45	43	31	26	23	19
32	46	47	35	29	25	21
33	47	50	40	32	27	23
34	48	54	45	35	29	25
35	49	59	50	38	31	27
36	50	63	54	42	34	30
37	51	67	58	46	38	34
38	52	70	62	50	42	39
39	53	73	66	55	46	42
40	54	76	70	59	50	45
41	55	79	73	61	53	47
42	56	81	75	63	55	50
43	57	83	77	65	57	52
44	58	85	79	67	59	55
45	59	87	81	70	61	57
46	60	88	83	73	64	60
47	61	90	85	76	66	62
48	62	91	87	78	68	64
49	62	92	89	80	70	65
50	63	93	90	82	72	67

Raw Score (Number Right)	T-Score Equivalent	Percentile Rank for each of five ages				
		11 yrs. 6 mos.	12 yrs. 6 mos.	13 yrs. 6 mos.	14 yrs. 6 mos.	15 yrs. 6 mos.
51	64	94	91	84	74	69
52	65	95	92	85	76	71
53	66	96	93	87	78	73
54	66	97	94	88	79	75
55	67	98	95	89	80	76
56	68	98	95	90	82	78
57	69	99	96	91	83	79
58	70	99	97	92	84	80
59	70	99	97	83	85	81
60	71		98	94	86	82
61	71		98	94	87	83
62	72		98	95	88	84
63	72		98	95	89	85
64	73		99	96	90	86
65	73		99	96	91	87
66	74			97	92	88
67	74			97	92	89
68	75			98	93	90
69	75			98	93	90
70	76			99	94	91
71	76				94	91
72	77				95	92
73	77				95	92
74	78				96	93
75	78				96	94
76	79				97	94
77	79				97	95
78	80				98	95
79	80				98	96
80	81				99	96
81	81					97
82	82					97
83	82					97
84	83					98
85	83					98
86	84					98
87	84					98
88	85					98
89	85					99
90	86					99
91	86					99
92	87					99
93	87					99
94	88					99
95	88					99
Median Number Right		33	35	38	40	42
Median T-Score		47	49	52	54	56

TABLE XVI. RAW SCORES (NUMBER RIGHT), T-SCORE EQUIVALENTS, AND PERCENTILE RANKS FOR EACH SCORE FOR EACH AGE FOR TEST II

Total Number Cases, 1087

Raw Score Number Right	T-Score Equivalent	Percentile Rank for each of six ages					
		10 yrs. 6 mos.	11 yrs. 6 mos.	12 yrs. 6 mos.	13 yrs. 6 mos.	14 yrs. 6 mos.	15 yrs. 6 mos.
1	20	1					
2	22	1					
3	24	1					
4	26	1					
5	28	2	1				
6	29	3	2	1			
7	30	4	2	1	1		
8	31	5	3	2	1		
9	32	6	4	2	1		
10	33	8	5	3	2	1	1
11	34	10	6	4	2	1	1
12	35	12	8	3	2	2	1
13	36	15	9	6	4	3	2
14	36	18	11	7	4	3	2
15	37	21	13	8	5	4	3
16	37	24	16	10	6	5	4
17	38	27	18	11	8	6	5
18	39	30	20	13	9	7	6
19	40	33	22	15	10	8	8
20	40	36	24	16	12	10	9
21	41	39	26	18	14	12	10
22	42	42	29	20	16	14	12
23	43	46	32	22	18	16	14
24	44	50	35	25	21	18	16
25	45	54	38	28	23	20	19
26	46	58	42	31	26	23	21
27	47	62	46	34	28	26	23
28	48	65	50	38	30	28	26
29	48	68	54	42	34	31	29
30	49	71	58	46	37	34	32
31	50	74	62	50	40	37	35
32	51	76	65	54	44	40	37
33	52	78	68	57	47	43	40
34	53	80	71	61	50	46	43
35	54	82	74	64	54	50	46
36	55	84	77	67	58	54	50
37	56	86	79	70	62	57	53
38	57	88	81	73	65	61	56
39	58	90	83	75	68	64	59
40	59	91	85	77	70	67	62
41	59	93	87	79	73	70	65
42	60	94	88	81	75	72	68

Raw Score (Number Right)	T-Score Equivalent	Percentile Rank for each of six ages					
		10 yrs. 6 mos.	11 yrs. 6 mos.	12 yrs. 6 mos.	13 yrs. 6 mos.	14 yrs. 6 mos.	15 yrs. 6 mos.
43	61	95	90	83	78	75	71
44	62	96	91	85	80	77	74
45	62	97	93	87	82	79	77
46	63	97	94	88	84	82	79
47	64	98	95	90	86	84	81
48	64	99	96	92	88	86	83
49	65	99.4	97	94	90	88	85
50	66	99.9	98	95	92	90	87
51	67		99	96	94	92	89
52	68		99.2	97	95	93	90
53	69		99.4	97	96	94	92
54	70		99.6	98	97	95	94
55	71		99.9	99	98	96	95
56	72			99.2	98	97	96
57	73			99.4	99	98	97
58	74			99.6	99.3	98	98
59	75			99.9	99.6	98	98
60	76				99.9	99	98
61	77					99.1	98
62	78					99.3	98
63	79					99.5	99
64	80					99.7	99
65	81					99.9	99.1
66	82						99.2
67	83						99.3
68	84						99.5
69	85						99.7
70	86						99.9
71	87						
72	87						
73	88						
74	88						
75	89						
76	89						
77	90						
78	90						
Median Number Right		24	28	31	34	35	36
Median T-Score		44	48	50	53	54	55

6

Form of Distribution for Picture Tests I and II. In order to convey an idea of the form of distribution for Picture Tests I and II for Grades 6, 7, and 8, the following figures are included. It will be noted that all these distributions conform fairly closely to the normal probability form. There is no reason to suppose the irregularities are not due to chance.

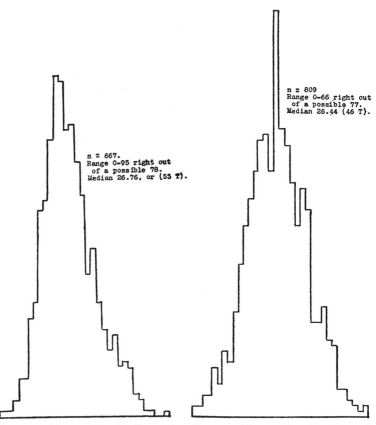

n = 809
Range 0-66 right out
of a possible 77.
Median 26.44 (46 T).

n = 667.
Range 0-95 right out
of a possible 78.
Median 26.76, or (53 T).

FIG. 12. Picture Test I. Form of Distribution for Grades 6, 7 and 8 Combined.

FIG. 13. Picture Test II. Form of Distribution for Grades 6, 7 and Combined.

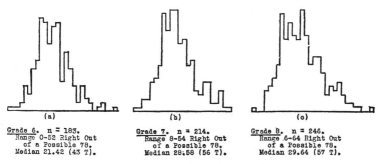

Grade 6. n = 183.
Range 0-52 Right Out
of a Possible 78.
Median 21.42 (43 T).

Grade 7. n = 214.
Range 8-54 Right Out
of a Possible 78.
Median 28.58 (56 T).

Grade 8. n = 246.
Range 6-64 Right Out
of a Possible 78.
Median 29.64 (57 T).

FIG. 14.   Picture Test I.   Form of Distribution for Grades 6, 7 and 8 Individually.

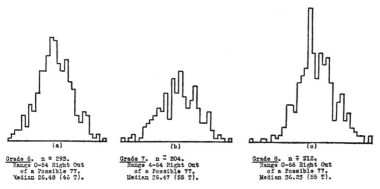

Grade 6. n = 293.
Range 0-54 Right Out
of a Possible 77.
Median 26.48 (46 T).

Grade 7. n = 204.
Range 4-64 Right Out
of a Possible 77.
Median 36.47 (55 T).

Grade 8. n = 312.
Range 0-66 Right Out
of a Possible 77.
Median 36.23 (55 T).

FIG. 15.   Picture Test II.   Form of Distribution for Grades 6, 7 and 8 Individually.

4. RELIABILITY OF PICTURE TESTS

As a measure of reliability of Test I, the first half was correlated with the second half. For 103 cases in Grades 6, 7 and 8, $r = .79$. For Test II, 200 unselected cases from Grades 6, 7 and 8 give coefficients as follows: Between Exercise 1 and Exercise 2, $r = .61$. Between Exercise 2 and Exercise 3, $r = .68$.   These coefficients of self-correlation are sufficiently high to be acceptable.   In correlating the scores in either of these tests with other scores, this reliability measure must be considered.   The effect of the unreliability is to reduce correlations, and also to increase the apparent amount of overlapping of age or grade groups.   The reliability of these tests compares favorably with that of others.

5. CORRELATIONS WITH ASSEMBLING TESTS AND WITH SHOP RANKS

The correlations of chief interest in the case of the picture tests are those with other criteria of mechanical ability. The best of these is the score in the assembling tests. Those computed are as follows:

TEST I WITH ASSEMBLING TEST I

	No.	r
6th, 7th and 8th grade boys, Lincoln School	27	.85
8th grade boys, New York City public schools	33	.59
8th grade boys, New York City public schools	35	.88
6th grade boys, New York City public schools	39	.44

TEST II WITH ASSEMBLING TEST I

5th, 6th, 7th and 8th grade boys, Lincoln School	50	.77
7th grade boys, New York City public schools	69	.45
8th grade boys, New York City public schools	30	.59
7th and 8th grade boys, Lincoln School	23	.82

The other criterion available is shop teachers' ranks. The coefficients found are:

TEST I WITH SHOP RANK

	No.	r
7th and 8th grade boys, Lincoln School	27	.83
High school boys (all years)	53	.53
6th and 7th grade boys	14	.51
6th grade boys	18	.59
6th grade boys	17	.59

TEST II WITH SHOP RANK

7th and 8th grade boys, Lincoln School	27	.84
6th and 7th grade boys, New York public schools	14	.43
6th grade boys, New York public schools	17	.65

The intercorrelations of Tests I and II are also of interest. The coefficients found are:

	No.	r
7th and 8th grade boys, Lincoln School	25	.88
5th, 6th, 7th, and 8th grade boys, New York City public schools	230	.68

It will be noted that the public schools' ranks always correlate lower than the private school ranks. This undoubtedly indicates that in the private schools where the classes are smaller their abilities are better known. We may accept the highest correlations as most nearly true, since all chance factors tend to reduce the correlation.

6. SUMMARY OF PICTURE TESTS OF MECHANICAL APTITUDE

The foregoing facts indicate that in these tests we have two useful instruments for detecting an ability which seems to be closely correlated with the ability to score in the assembling tests, and with qualities which lead shop teachers to rank pupils high or low. It is, therefore, entirely justifiable to assume in general that a high score in the picture tests is an indication of general mechanical aptitude. To obtain the best measure, both the assembling tests and the picture tests, are advisable. For preliminary classification, however, the picture tests alone may serve. The most obvious query that occurs in comparing the assembling tests and the picture tests is somewhat as follows:

"May a child not be expert with his fingers and be able to score high in working with actual materials and still have but little knowledge of the kind called for in the picture tests, or vice versa?"

The answer is of course to be found in our correlations. These range as high as .88 between the Assembling Series and the Picture Tests, which means that there is a very marked tendency for these two traits to be found together. This is not equivalent to saying that the two kinds of tests measure exactly the same traits. The difference between the obtained correlation and perfect correlation is a measure of the extent to which one trait occurs without the other.

The ease with which these picture tests can be given and scored will be the chief reason for substituting them for the assembling series.

PART II

THE NEED FOR A BROADER DEFINITION OF GENERAL INTELLIGENCE

Section XVIII

Illustrious School Failures

Cases in which illustrious (not to include "merely successful") men and women were, while in school, diagnosed as failures by their teachers have been often cited. Many of the men and women who later became world authorities in their fields, were called at best but mediocre. Linnaeous' gymnasium teacher told his father that he was unfit for any profession. Yet this boy later was to revolutionize the science of botany.[1] Charles Darwin says in his autobiography that he "was considered by all his masters and by his father as a very ordinary boy, rather below the common standard of intellect." Napoleon Bonaparte in the final examination at his military school stood forty-second in his class. We may well ask with Swift, "Who were the forty-one above him?" Robert Fulton was called a dullard because his mind seemed filled with things outside of school. Priestly, the great chemist, had "an exceedingly imperfect education." Pasteur "was not at all remarkable at school. Books and study had little attraction for him." M. Pierre Curie, late professor of physics at the University of Paris, and co-discoverer with his wife of radium, "was so stupid in school that his parents removed him and placed him under a private tutor." Such a list as this could, if space permitted, be continued to great length. Many men who to-day are national or world figures, but who had a poor school record, could be cited.

Granting that these cases constitute but a minority, and granting also a certain tendency to exaggeration by biographers who love contrasts, these cases are still too numerous and important to be ignored. The fundamental fact remains that the abilities

---

[1] Citations are from Swift: *Mind in the Making*, Chap. I.

of many pupils are widely misjudged in school, and the abilities displayed either unperceived or misunderstood because of arrested development, poorly suited courses, stereotyped curricula, and general lack of sufficiently broad means for estimating ability.

No claim is here made that *all* so-called low I.Q.'s are misjudged — only that *many* are.

SECTION XIX

THE LARGE PERCENTAGE OF "LOW INTELLIGENCE"

That a great majority of pupils who enter the first grade drop out even before the end of first year high school is well known. Strayer's study of 318 cities, quoted by Terman, shows that of those who enter the first grade, on the average only 37 per cent enter first year high school, 25 per cent enter second year high school, 17 per cent enter third year high school and 14 per cent enter fourth year high school. Studies by Ayers and Thorndike also show the same general tendency. Terman says, "It is not uncommon for one-third to drop out without finishing the first year of high school." Retardation and elimination figures from every city offer annually additional testimony of the same general facts in elementary as well as high school. Terman believes that "not all of this elimination is traceable to inferior mental ability, but that a large part is due to this cause there is no longer room for doubt." With this general statement all will of course agree. The question, however, of just how much is due to actual lack of intelligence in its broadest sense, we do not know. Terman presents much evidence to show that with the use of the general intelligence tests pupils who have low intelligence and who will drop out can be largely discovered beforehand.

But a situation in which over 80 per cent of the pupil population is eliminated before they reach their goal, is not greatly helped by the statement that most of the pupils who thus are eliminated haven't the general intelligence to proceed further. Is it not rather an indictment both of the curricula, and of the tests which select largely on identical bases? Terman suggests the query, "Are high school standards too high?" We might also ask are they too narrow? Or, in general, too far removed from the kinds of mental capacities of pupils?

If such great numbers of the school population haven't the kind of ability we call general intelligence, why call it general?

Fortunately there now seems to be a tendency to scrutinize more closely the nature of the courses offered as well as the abilities of the pupils.

Section XX
What Is General Intelligence?

Certain it is that the term general intelligence is sorely in need of definition, for by the average person, and even a large number of specialists in educational measurement, it is accepted at face value to mean just what it says. But is it not a loose use of terms that permits us to use the name "general" intelligence to designate mental traits which are painstakingly limited to the literary-academic tasks of our present intelligence tests? Are we not misleading when we say that he, and (in effect) *only* he has general intelligence, who with paper and pencil can effectively do such things as, for example, solve simple problems in arithmetic, state the opposites for each of a list of words, fill in a number of deleted sentences, arrange words in certain logical relationships, decide whether a given number or word is identical with another; or write the seventh letter of the alphabet, arrange a jumble of words to form meaningful sentences, make a cross that "shall be in the circle but not in the triangle or square; state which day comes before Sunday; or write whether a sentinel should be trustworthy, whether alliteration is a form of pentameter, whether cessation of belligerency is ever desirable; or state "what one should do if it is raining when we start to school," or repeat "we are having a fine time. We found a little mouse in the trap," or repeat "3-1-7-5-9," or give the greatest possible number of words in one minute which rhyme with "day," or any combination of such tasks that may occupy the 30 to 45 minutes, given to an average present-day intelligence test?

What sort of mentality has the individual who makes a low score in such tasks but who when he drops out of school has the ability to organize a gang that is all but indissolvable? Or who drops out of school and builds up a world-wide business on the identical ground where "brighter" men have failed? Or who can wrest from a Robinson Crusoe situation a triumphant career? Or even he who can start a balking automobile abandoned by "superior" persons—men of higher I.Q.'s? Or what shall we say

79

for the lamented low intelligence of the New York boy who escaped from an institution for mental defectives and who before the authorities recaptured him had obtained and was holding a job paying him thirty-seven do'lars per week?

To say that there are but few such cases is untrue, for even though the illustrious cases do constitute but a small minority, who shall estimate how many more of that large percentage who drop out of school, because it is unsuited to their needs, would develop into careers of marked usefulness, if their real abilities were discovered?

To say that such persons as those cited (except, perhaps, such cases as the last mentioned) are not possessed of general intelligence is to quarrel with words. Though they may classify as "low I.Q.'s" by present-day intelligence tests, surely we are on uncertain ground if we take such results at face value and consider their cases closed.

It is a question of what our tests measure, a question of what we mean to include under the term general intelligence.

If we examine the type of criteria by which nearly all these tests are justified, we find that these consist in the last analysis essentially óf teachers' estimates of pupils' ability in school, plus records in other academic tests. But our major contention is precisely that for many children the teachers' estimates and their academic record is merely an estimate of success in bookish tasks, and here it is that fallacies of intelligence ratings creep in.

It is submitted that these intelligence tests, at best, detect only those academic qualities of pupils which are noted by teachers, and which, it is freely granted, are of great importance for success in ordinary school curricula, but which do not constitute the whole of general intelligence. Of this our abler investigators[1] are fully aware, but the average giver of tests is not aware of it,—or, if so,—overlooks it.

---

[1] See Thorndike: "Tests of Intelligence, Reliability, Significance, etc.," *School and Society*, Vol. IX, Feb. 15, 1919, and Henmon, "Measurement of Intelligence," *ibid.*, Vol. XIII, Feb. 5, 1921.

Section XXI

Other Kinds of Intelligence

As a matter of fact, it seems clear that intelligence may be classified as of many kinds. Thus, for example, the campaign manager exhibits a quality differing sharply from that of the locomotive engineer; while the kind of intelligence required to lay out the construction work of a Woolworth Building is not very like that needed to write a forceful letter, and this in turn is not very like that employed in painting a great picture, inventing a great engine—or modern linotype.

While it may be true that a certain minimum body of "sense," mental agility, and some general academic information underlies all such activities, we know from at least a few correlations obtained (one of which appears later) that the relationship is not very close—though it is, to be sure, positive.

If we had trustworthy criteria of ability in social leadership and in the various political and mechanical arts and sciences, it might be possible to devise intelligence tests that would be more nearly "general" than those we now have. This, however, is a more difficult matter than to devise tests of academic ability. Again, while to measure in this wide sense the present ability of our school population represents a heavy task,—to prognosticate its *potential* ability would truly be a Herculean undertaking. But this is not equivalent to saying that it can't be done. Much of the same methodology and technique which we already have would probably apply, and progress in this direction may be looked for. Current literature is already sprinkled with discussions of the limitations of what our present so-called general intelligence tests measure. While unfortunately much of the criticism of intelligence tests emanates from self-appointed critics, incompetent for the most part to pass scientifically upon their merits or shortcomings, the best authorities, and many of the authors of the tests themselves, are well aware that more comprehensive and more valid instruments are urgently needed. "Compared to what we should like to have they are very faulty. Compared to what they replace, however, they may be notably superior."

SECTION XXII

GENERAL INTELLIGENCE AND MECHANICAL ABILITY

The tests of mechanical ability herein described may serve as an example and case in point, showing a type of intelligence and also emphasizing the need for clearer definition of just what we mean when we say a child has but little general intelligence.

During 1919–20 several hundred boys in a New York City public school (P. S. 64, Manhattan) were given a very exhaustive intelligence rating by means of the combined results in the following well known tests.[1]

I. THE INTELLIGENCE TESTS

The intelligence tests used in the study were:

1. National Intelligence Test A
2. National Intelligence Test B
3. Haggerty Intelligence Test Delta 2
4. Otis Intelligence Test
5. Meyers Mental Measure
6. Thorndike Visual Vocabulary Scale

The results of these six tests were pooled, giving equal weight to each, and the final rating called the composite intelligence score. These boys were next given a series of mechanical tests, consisting of the following.

2. THE MECHANICAL TESTS

The mechanical tests used in the study were:

1. Assembling Series 1
2. Assembling Series 2
3. Picture Test I
4. Picture Test II

The detailed nature of each of these mechanical tests has been previously given.

---

[1] For full report see Stenquist (J. L.), "Better Grading through Standard Mental Tests," *Bureau of Reference, Research and Statistics Bulletin*, 1921.

If we now compare the results in the two types of examination we may observe the following points for this group.

In the correlation between the Assembling Test, Series I, and

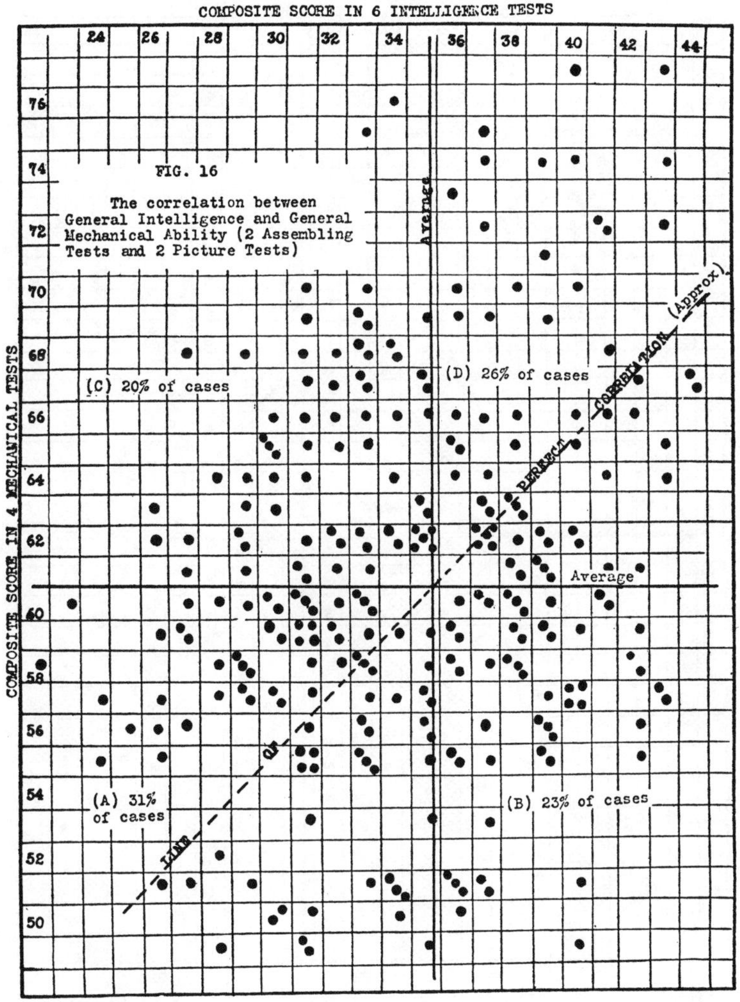

FIG. 16

The correlation between General Intelligence and General Mechanical Ability (2 Assembling Tests and 2 Picture Tests)

the composite intelligence score, $r = .230 \pm .04$ for 267 7th and 8th grade boys (Fig. 17). Between Assembling Test, Series II, and the composite intelligence score, $r = .338 \pm .06$ for 100 7th and 8th grade boys. Between Picture Test I and the same intelligence rating, $r = .52 \pm .07$ for 50 6th, 7th and 8th grade boys. Between Picture Test II and the same intelligence rating, $r = .64 \pm .06$ for 520 6th, 7th and 8th grade boys. (See Fig. 18.)

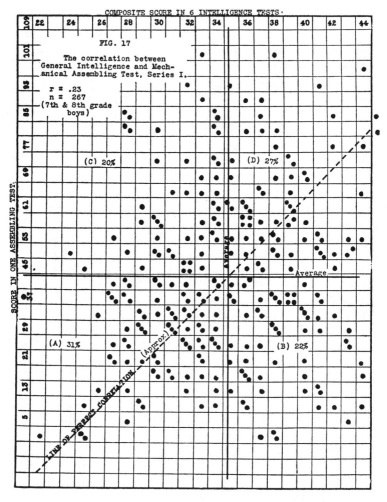

FIG. 17

The correlation between General Intelligence and Mechanical Assembling Test, Series I.

$r = .23$
$n = 267$
(7th & 8th grade boys)

If we now combine all of the four mechanical tests into one average T-score, and correlate it with the same intelligence rating, we find r drops to $.21 \pm .07$ for 275 7th and 8th grade boys. (See Fig. 16.)

The important inference to draw from these results is not with regard to the exact coefficients obtained, but with regard to the general fact of low correlation between the two kinds of ability here represented. Results obtained in the Army for over 14,000

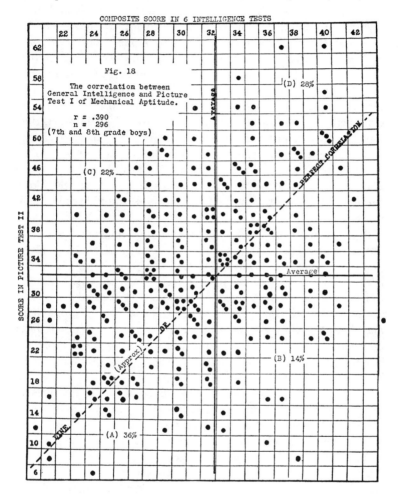

COMPOSITE SCORE IN 6 INTELLIGENCE TESTS

Fig. 18

The correlation between General Intelligence and Picture Test I of Mechanical Aptitude.

r = .390
n = 296
(7th and 8th grade boys)

men bear out the same general fact.[1]

An individual's position in General Intelligence is thus shown to be largely independent of his position in General Mechanical Ability and Aptitude.

---

[1] See page 58.

Analysis of Total Distribution. Examination of Fig. 16, which for convenience has been divided into quadrants each lettered, showing per cent of pupils included, shows that of the total cases, all in Groups A and C are *below* average in general intelligence, but all in Group C, or 20 per cent, are *above* average ability in the mechanical tests. All the pupils in both Groups C and D, or 46 per cent, are above average in mechanical ability. Of these 26 per cent are also above in general intelligence. But for the mechanical tests showing their marked ability in this direction also, it is unlikely that many of Group D would be encouraged to look toward careers in mechanical fields, since they have marked abstract intelligence. Conversely, those in Group B would not be known to be deficient in mechanical ability, though above average in intelligence. Considering mechanical ability alone we may say that Groups C and D would likely succeed in this direction, while Groups A and B would not be likely to do so.

Again, if we were to rely merely on the intelligence tests all in Group C would fail to be recognized as having ability, although 55 pupils, or 20 per cent, have ability of the other kind. Consider next·Group A, who are low in both tests: It is not without value to have this double negative information. At least advice can be given less blindly than without such information. Again, there may be quite different types of abilities in which some of these may excel. Having them segregated we can proceed more intelligently than otherwise, to say the least. Less progress should be looked for, for one thing.

In short, the mechanical tests have given us important clues as to abilities which would not be revealed by the abstract intelligence tests alone. Though the correlation is positive it is so low as to permit wide differences in deviation. These are the measure of abilities untouched by so-called general intelligence tests.

The Trustworthiness of the Measurements. As regards the reliability of our measure of general intelligence: Comprised as it is of six excellent tests, say *one* of which would generally be accepted as a measure of general intelligence, constitutes an unimpeachable estimate of that type of ability which we now call general intelligence. In mechanical ability we have repeated tests of each of two types of mechanical tasks,—the assembling tests involving skill, and the picture tests involving mechanical information and reasoning, i.e., we have in fact four distinct measurements of each pupil. The reliability of our measures is, therefore, acceptable, and much better than is generally obtainable.

The Validity of the Measurements. The validity of a test deals with the question of what it is that it measures,—i.e., with correlations with criteria.

The question of what the intelligence tests measure has already been dealt with in Section XX. As to what the mechanical tests measure we may cite the correlations which have been found in comparing mechanical test scores with pupils' rank in shop courses, or in general science courses, as given on pages 59 and 74.

These correlations are all subject to chance errors *which reduce them.* The true correlations are therefore higher,—probably .7 or higher.

Shop teachers' ranks are of course no better than regular teachers' ranks which have been attacked in a previous section. But there is every reason to believe them *equally good.* Were other and better criteria available these would be excluded. In several of the above instances, however, only the average rank given by two shop teachers (intercorrelating .88 or better) were used.

The mechanical tests may, therefore, be judged from these figures to detect to a marked degree the same qualities in pupils that are considered by shop and science teachers in judging pupils' relative abilities.

The second way of deciding what these mechanical tests measure is the very direct one of merely looking at the tests and judging what type of task it is that has been set up. Thus we may note at once that they represent an attempt (in all except Picture Test II) to get away from words. They deal with concrete and real things, as against description of things. In the case of the Assembling Test it gives opportunity to do with hands and mind, rather than to perform with a pencil only, or to juggle mental abstractions.

It may be thought, however, that the mixture of abilities revealed by combining picture and assembling tests is less illuminating than would be either taken alone. To observe this point the records in one assembling test were plotted separately. These appear in Fig. 17. Strangely enough, the percentages in each quadrant is practically identical, with the correlation co-

7

efficient .23 as compared with .21 in the former case.   The form of distribution is very similar.   The same interpretations may, therefore, be made whether we employ Fig. 16 or Fig. 17.

In the same way the results of Picture Test II were plotted in Fig. 18.   Here the higher correlation is apparent.   The two tests are measuring more nearly the same kind of ability.

Section XXIII

The Relative Importance of These Two Kinds of Ability

Of the relative importance of each of these two types of ability readers must form their own conclusions. But it should be kept in mind that we are living in a world that is dominated on every hand by every form of mechanical device and machine. Every moment of present-day life is influenced directly or indirectly by the products of mechanical skill and genius. Is it not important that ability in this field should be discovered and developed? Rather than merely to dismiss our apparently stupid pupils as low in what we now call general intelligence, and to relegate them to some convenient class, might not our time profitably be spent in disclosing other kinds of intelligence of which they may be possessed?

The question of "what knowledge is of most worth" will probably never be finally answered to the satisfaction of all. But it seems certain that as life becomes more and more complex, the world's tasks become more varied, and group inter-dependence increases, there is constant need for broader conceptions of what constitutes worth-while mental ability. We should recall that the history of the past century, as has often been said, could well be written in terms of the achievement of applied science and applied mechanical genius. Inventions of hitherto undreamed of significance, which have revolutionized or at least profoundly influenced the life of every nation on the globe, have sprung from this field of knowledge. And while the attempts to measure the mental abilities back of these forces, which are herein described, represent but crude beginnings, the importance of the task is stoutly maintained. Indeed, to explore, measure and adequately capitalize these capacities seems at least as important as doing the same for the more abstract type intelligence required in academic school subjects. The discovery of special abilities has a two-fold significance and like the quality of mercy "is twice blessed": It not only opens the door of new promise to pupils, many of whom have been labelled as failures, but in doing so it leads toward further contributions to society.

Section XXIV

Fictitious Stigmas

There is a more or less universal notion that a low score in such tasks as have here been called intelligence tests constitutes a disgrace that must be shunned at all costs. To fail to receive a high rating in intelligence is most deplorable—a great calamity. This feeling has come about partly through the loose use of the term general intelligence, and partly through distorted estimate of the rôle of intelligence in human conduct. But, absurd as it may seem, there is a brief, and a reasonable one, which can be held for the pupil with an actual low I.Q. as well as for the one with a supposed low I.Q. For just as in man we find enormous individual differences in intelligence, so (fortunately) in the work of the world we find equally great variation in the character of the various tasks. As a matter of fact, the outstanding industrial tendency of the past decade has been to reduce the number of skilled jobs and increase the number of unskilled ones. The constant tendency of our modern machine age is in this direction, be it right or wrong. Again, consider the hundreds of thousands of menial tasks outside of industry that somebody in every society must perform. Is it not clear that happiness, contentment and efficiency in such jobs are far more apt to come with a *low* I.Q. than with one that is high? Indeed, even when we consider the world's sweetest and most lovable characters, it is not always their high general abstract intelligence that makes the strongest appeal. Haven't we in the academic atmosphere of our school rooms come to value the intellectual side of human nature out of proportion to its real significance in life? Surely far worse calamities can befall the human animal than that being pronounced as of low intelligence. Physical disease, a crippled body, an insane or actually feeble mind, with the multitude of tragic afflictions which this may imply—these and many other lamentable conditions which may befall should be kept in the background of our mind when we feel inclined to bemoan the lot of the stupid individual.

SECTION XXV

SUMMARY OF PART II

Part II attempts to point out some of the fallacies that are prevalent in the present-day considerations of mental tests. It recalls the many cases of illustrious men who were called school failures, and calls attention to the large percentages of pupils who at present appear to lack sufficient mentality to carry on current curricula, and suggests the query, "Is it the curricula or the mental ability of the population that is at fault?" It criticizes present-day intelligence tests as narrow and academic in scope, being based largely on school success, shows the loose use to which the term "general intelligence" is often put, and maintains that there are in fact very likely many other kinds of intelligence than that measured by the tests given that name. As an illustration the results of a study of mechanical ability are offered. Here it is shown that at least 40 per cent of the pupils from a typical school, who are below average in general abstract intelligence, are *above* average in the kind of ability required in four mechanical tests, the detailed nature of which is described. It is submitted that such ability may be of quite as general importance as that required to score high in the abstract general intelligence tests, in view of the fact that present environment is so largely permeated with the fruits of mechanical genius and applied science. Finally, it is maintained that there is a strong, but wrong tendency to attach a stigma to pupils scoring low in these so-called general intelligence tests. Even for those pupils whose true general intelligence is found actually low,—after adequate tests (many being only apparently low)—even for these ample ground exists for hopes of a useful and happy life doing tasks for which they are, in fact, better adapted than are individuals of high intelligence. Attention is called to the fact that just as we find very great individual differences in the abilities of human beings, so we find (fortunately) very wide variation in the types of the world's work which is to be done; and that if the kind and degree of abilities possessed by an individual are discovered and properly capitalized, it should be possible to find appropriate opportunities for every one.

APPENDIX

ASSEMBLING TESTS

1. DIRECTIONS FOR GIVING AND SCORING

1. (*a*) GENERAL MANAGEMENT:

Boxes are always handled in strap carriers; bundles of 8 or 10 can easily be moved about. Caution pupils to be careful not to drop boxes or parts. If a part should be lost from a box, place a protruding slip of paper in the compartment from which it is missing. Such box can then be identified instantly, and repaired later. Series I yellow tags; Series II green tags.

(*b*) TO GIVE TEST:

Use regular classroom, and single desks, if possible. With pupils seated, and 40 to 50 boxes, and also score sheets, near the examiner's desk, proceed as follows:

1. Distribute score sheets, one for each pupil. (Make sure you have the right ones.) Each pupil fills out score sheet blanks—name, age, etc.—and leaves blank on his desk *to be enclosed in the box when he finishes.* (If he fails to enclose it there is no way of identifying his box.)

2. Appoint one boy for each row to distribute boxes to each row. *Do not permit the boxes to be opened until all begin.*

3. When each pupil has his box instruct as follows: "We will now read the directions; you read them, but not aloud. (Examiner now takes one box and reads the directions on box aloud, while the pupils read silently.) As soon as examiner has finished, and all understand, he says, "You have 30 minutes; all ready, begin."

Note that boxes open backward. See that all get started right, beginning with Model A, B, etc. After about 3 minutes say again, "Do not spend more than about 3 minutes on any one model." Examiner should write down the time of beginning, being careful to allow just 30 minutes.

4. When time is up, each pupil hands in his box (*with record sheet inside*). Stack the boxes immediately beside the scorer's desk if they are to be scored at once.

(*c*) FINISHING BEFORE 30 MINUTES ARE UP:

A few extra-skilled pupils will finish before 30 minutes have elapsed. Have them mark the time spent on their record sheet, and allow each such record one-half point for each minute remaining up to 30—e.g., 22 minutes spent plus 8/2, that is, 4 would be added to the score.

92

(*d*) SCORING:

Select two or three pupils, who appeared to be doing the best in the test, as assistants. With boxes conveniently stacked beside his desk examiner-scorer proceeds as follows:

1. Sit down at desk. Take one box, open (cover *toward* you). Unfold Record Sheet. Now *inspect* Model A, and write score on Record Sheet. *Inspect* Model B, and write score on Record Sheet. Do the same for all models. When you have entered a score for each model, pass the box to your first assistant, who takes each model apart, being very careful that no parts are missing, and that no model is overlooked. (The examiner will need to instruct his assistants once or twice for each model, after which they can disassemble models quite as well as he can. But the examiner must continually *emphasize* the importance of *extremely accurate inspection*—to see that all parts and all models are O. K.)

2. Proceed in the same way with all the boxes. After a little practice this process can be done at high speed, so that a whole class can be scored in a few minutes.

To save lost motion the assistants stack the boxes directly on the strap carriers, when they finish disassembling. Thus one bundle (of 10) after another is finished, and strapped up ready for use again.

Note: After the boy assistants have become *very expert*, it is permissible to train *a very few* of them to do the actual inspecting, that is, to actually enter the scores, on the record sheets, as official scorers. This must, however, be closely controlled by the teacher in charge, who will be responsible.

2. DETAILS OF GIVING PARTIAL SCORES

In the standard score sheets for each of Series I, II, and III, the partial score values for various degrees of perfection in each model are listed as plus or minus values, which are simply points above 0 (every model is graded 0, 1, 2, 3, 4, 5, 6, 7, 8, 9 or 10) or below 10. Minus values are used because it is often more clear to "deduct" for a certain mistake than to "credit" for the partial solution. A sample record is shown on page 98.

While these partial score values appear troublesome at first glance, they are quickly memorized, and after practice with a class or two, it may not be necessary even to consult the list of values. Occasionally new combinations of parts of models appear, which are not listed. These need give the scorer no great concern. He should assign what seems (in terms of the other partial values) a reasonable score value. The justification for this is that these small variations in partial scores affect but slightly the final score, because of the method of scoring.

When each model has been given an individual raw score add these up, look up the equivalent T-Scale score in the proper table [1] and enter this T-Scale score in proper place under "Final Score." This can all be done very rapidly with a little practice and with assistance as suggested under "Directions for Giving and Scoring," above.

---

[1] Pages 95 or 98.

3. THE SHORT FORM METHOD—SCORING NUMBER RIGHT ONLY

For many purposes it will be found entirely adequate to disregard partial scores and to count only the models solved perfectly. A large number of correlations between the two methods of scoring results in an average coefficient of between .8 and .9. A good plan when practicable is to give both Series I and Series II, when scoring by the number right method. This gives a more reliable sampling, and minimizes the work of scoring. In utilizing this method of scoring *all values of 8 and 9 as well as 10 are counted as right.*

4. RAW SCORES AND FINAL T–SCORES

The total number right (including the total of all partial score values, if the partial score method of scoring which is the more reliable, is used) plus any time credit which may be due, is the raw score. For each raw score the final T-Scale score appears in the table. This should be entered as pointed out above as the final score. The T-Scale scores are the mean square Deviation Equivalents for the distribution of 12-year-old boys, as has been explained on page 43. Tables I and II not only give the T-Score values, but also the age distributions for several ages, making possible an adequate definition of what a certain T-Score means.

5. NORMS

The median scores for each age constitute the Norms, for the maximum of scores available at time of this publication (February 1921).[1]

6. FURTHER DETAILS OF SCORING, AND HOW TO INTERPRET WHAT THE SCORES MEAN

On the opposite page appears a sample Standard Score Sheet for Series I. Each pupil to be tested first fills in the heading on one such blank, and when he has completed his work with the box, the score sheet is folded lengthwise and placed inside the box for identification. When scoring the examiner then writes 10 under "individual raw score" for each model properly assembled, and whatever partial score (from 1 to 9) for models only partially assembled.

INTERPRETATION OF A SAMPLE SCORE

Suppose the record for John Brown, who is 12 years old, to be as follows:

	Raw Score
Model A, (perfect)	10
Model B, (perfect)	10
Model C,	8
Model D, (perfect)	10
Model E,	4
Model F,	0
Model G,	0
Model H,	0
Model I,	0
Model J,	0
Total	42
Time Bonus	0
Total Raw Score	42

[1] See pages 45–46.

By consulting the table [1] the T-Score is found to be 56. Referring now to Table IX we find the following facts: A T-Score of 56 is equalled or exceeded by only 20.8 per cent of 12-year-old boys; by only 43.2 per cent of 13-year old boys; by 46.8 per cent of 14-year-olds, and by 75 per cent of adult men in the Army. We may also note the medians for each age at the foot of Table IX. These show that our score of 56 is exactly equal to the 14-year-old median. This gives us a well-defined notion of what it means. It shows just where John Brown stands in relation to boys of his own age as well as to those much older than he is.

The same interpretation may of course be made for any score in any of the Series. Any standard of performance can also be set up for any special purpose. Thus for example it may be desired to select for certain reasons all pupils who score higher than 75 per cent of 12-year-olds in general," or "all who score lower than 50 per cent of 13-year-olds in general," etc.

7. TO BE USED AS A GROUP TEST

Each series is designed to be used as a class test, it being more practicable to test an entire class than a single pupil. In order to facilitate this the outfits have all been made up in one standard size. The uniform boxes are easily handled by means of special strap carriers, eight or ten such outfits when strapped up being not materially more difficult to handle than an ordinary suitcase. The outfits can of course be used over and over again.

Full directions are printed on each box. These are read aloud by the examiner and silently by the pupils.

At first thought it may appear that the expense involved is too great to use these tests as group tests. But it should be remembered the expense of time necessary in individual testing *is far greater* than the cost of apparatus, not to mention the general impracticability of the method, in public schools. It should also be kept in mind that sets of 40 to 50 of these tests, for testing entire classes can be used continuously, and should be considered as permanent equipment. If the mental measurement of children is worth obtaining it is worth providing the necessary materials, for great pains have been taken in devising these tests to make them essentially group tests. In the Army entire companies were tested at once.

---

[1] At margin of standard score sheet.

SAMPLE SCORE SHEET

SERIES I

Name .... Age......................
(Nearest Birthday)

Grade.................. School.......................

FINAL
T-SCORE:

STANDARD SCORE SHEET
STENQUIST ASSEMBLING TEST

[ ]

SERIES I

Individual
Raw
Score:

NOTE: Do not fail to place this record inside box when you have finished the test. FOLD LENGTHWISE.

Raw Score	"T" Score
0 to 1	24
2 to 3	30
4 to 5	31
6 to 7	33
8 to 9	35
10 to 11	38
12 to 13	40
14 to 15	42
16 to 17	43
18 to 19	44
20 to 21	45
22 to 23	46
24 to 25	47
26 to 27	48
28 to 29	49
30 to 31	50
32 to 33	51
34 to 35	52
36 to 37	53
38 to 39	54
40 to 41	55
42 to 43	56
44 to 45	57
46 to 47	58
48 to 49	59
50 to 51	60
52 to 53	60
54 to 55	61
56 to 57	62
58 to 59	62
60 to 61	63
62 to 63	64
64 to 65	64
66 to 67	65
68 to 69	66
70 to 71	67
72 to 73	68
74 to 75	68
76 to 77	69
78 to 79	70
80 to 81	72
82 to 83	74
84 to 85	74
86 to 87	75
88 to 89	75
90 to 91	79
92 to 93	80
94 to 95	80
96 to 97	81
98 to 99	81
100 to ..	82

Model A

Cupboard Catch. Spring wrong = —5; Knob wrong = —5; Bolt wrong = —5.

Model B

Clothes Pin. Spring properly placed on 1 stick = +2. Spring placed at end of one or both sticks = +2.

Model C

Paper Clip (Hunt). 1 lever properly in slot, but reversed = +2. Both levers properly in slot, but reversed = +8. Both levers backward in slot = +2. All other combinations = 0.

Model D

Chain. For each pair of links properly joined, +2; any number of links only half (singly) joined, +2; All other combinations = 0.

Model E

Bicycle Bell. Thumb lever on pin, reversed = +1; Correct = +2. Gear on pin, reversed = +1; correct = +2. Knocker on pin, inverted = +1; correct = +2. Spring hooked properly = +4.

Model F

Rubber Hose Shut-Off. Thumb lever above spring backward = +8; Thumb lever inserted under spring, any position = +2.

Model G

Wire Bottle Stopper. Rubber stop in place = +1. The two heavy wires properly connected = +4. Small wire properly connected = +5.

Model H

Push Button. Button right = +1. Button disk upside down, all else O. K. = +4. All O. K. except not snapped = +6.

Model I

Lock. Lug in place = +4; Bolt in place = +1. Spring in place = +4. Cover in place with screw = +1.

Model J

Mouse Trap. All right except one spring = +7; Both springs wrong, otherwise right = +4; Only loop-lever, pin, and bait-trigger right = +2; Only loop-lever and pin right = +1.

TIME BONUS..........
TOTAL
RAW SCORE..........

NOTE TO SCORER: Score all perfectly assembled models 10. "—" means deduct from 10. "+" means add to zero.

SAMPLE SCORE SHEET

SERIES II

Name.. Age.........................

(Nearest Birthday)

Grade.................. School......................

STANDARD SCORE SHEET
STENQUIST ASSEMBLING TEST

FINAL
"T" SCORE:

SERIES II

NOTE: Do not fail to place this record inside box when you
have finished the test. FOLD LENGTHWISE.

Individual
Raw
Score

	Raw Score	"T" Score
Model A. Pistol.	0 to 1	27
Two sides properly joined with screw = —1; Hammer in place = +2; Spring in proper position = +7.	2 to 3	29
	4 to 5	32
	6 to 7	35
Model B. Elbow Catch.	.8 to 9	37
Catch in place = +3. Spring in place = +3. Pin in place = +3.	10 to 11	39
	12 to 13	41
Model C. Rope Coupling.	14 to 15	42
Castings properly joined with screws = +1; Center stud properly in place = +5.	16 to 17	44
	18 to 19	45
	20 to 21	46
Model D. Expansion Nut.	22 to 23	47
Rings in place and sides O. K. = +4; Nut reversed or bolt reversed = —6.	24 to 25	48
	26 to 27	49
	28 to 29	50
Model E. Sash Fastener.	30 to 31	51
Top and Bottom in place, with screw in place, nut down = +3; Same, with nut up = +2, 1 spring in place = +4; Both springs in place = +5.	32 to 33	52
	34 to 35	54
	36 to 37	55
	38 to 39	55
Model F. Expansion Rubber Stopper.	40 to 41	56
Rubber properly on cone— +6. Bolt upside down = —4; nut wrong = —5.	42 to 43	57
	44 to 45	58
	46 to 47	58
Model G. Calipers.	48 to 49	59
Spring in place on both arms with adjusting screw in place of eye = +5; Pivot in place = +2. Sleeve in place = +1.	50 to 51	60
	52 to 53	61
	54 to 55	61
	56 to 57	62
Model H. Paper Clip.	58 to 59	63
Spring in place on jaws = +2; Pin inserted properly = +6; Pin inserted improperly = +1.	60 to 61	64
	62 to 63	65
	64 to 65	66
Model I. Double Acting Hinge.	66 to 67	67
For each pin in proper place = +1.	68 to 69	68
	70 to 71	70
	72 to 73	70
Model J. Lock No. 2.	74 to 75	71
Bolt in place = +1. Lug in place = +1. Both in place = +4; Spring in place = +6; Cover in place = +1.	76 to 77	72
	78 to 79	74
	80 to 81	74
	82 to 83	77

TIME BONUS .... NOTE TO SCORER: Score all perfectly
TOTAL assembled models 10. "—" means deduct
RAW SCORE........... from 10. "+" means "add to zero."

Raw Score	"T" Score
84 to 85	77
86 to 87	78
88 to 89	78
90 to 91	80
92 to 93	82

SAMPLE SCORE SHEET

Series III (Tentative)

Name . . . .   Age . . . .

(Nearest Birthday)

Grade . . . .   School . . . .   Date of Birth . . . .

SCORE SHEET

STENQUIST ASSEMBLING TEST

TIME . . . .   SERIES III

(If less than standard)   (For Grades 2, 3, 4, 5 and 6)

NOTE: Place this sheet inside the box when you have finished.   Fold lengthwise.

SCORES: Model A.   Plain Bolt and Nut

No partial score.   Right or wrong.   Not necessary to screw nut up tight.   Score: 0 or 10

Model B.—Bolt and Wing Nut.   (Perfect Score = 10.)

Nut reversed = plus 2 only.

Model C.—Plain Hinge.   (Perfect Score = 10.)

Two halves joined, but one part inverted: plus 2.   Pin inserted in one part only = 0.   Score: 0, 2 or 10.

Model D.—Key and Ring.   (Perfect Score = 10.)

Key only half on ring = plus 2.   No attempt = 0.

Model E.—Turn Buckle.   (Perfect Score = 10.)

Screw eyes properly in one end only = plus 2.   Not necessary to screw up tight.

Model F.—Drawer Pull.   (Perfect Score = 10.)

Washer wrong in any way, subtract 5.   Finished surface on wrong side, subtract 4.

Model G.—Trunk Caster.   (Perfect Score = 10.)

For failure to push pin clear through, subtract 8.

Model H.—Plain Push Button.   (Perfect Score = 10.)

For button out of place, subtract 6.   Parts merely laid together (not screwed up) score 1 only.

Model I.—Belt and Buckle.   (Perfect Score = 20.)

Permanent end properly fastened, score 10.   Loose end properly buckled, score 5. Strap not reversed (right side out) credit 5.   Subtract same amounts for each step wrong.

Model J.—Nail Clip.   (Perfect Score = 20.)

Jaws and pin properly in place, score 10.   Spring properly in place, 10.   Spring reversed,   5.

TOTAL

SCORE:

MECHANICAL APTITUDE TESTS

INSTRUCTIONS FOR GIVING TEST I

Pupils must be seated so as to prevent copying.

Desks are cleared, pencils provided, and monitors pass out booklets, one to each pupil.

Examiner instructs all pupils to fill in properly the heading on the blanks, being especially careful to obtain the correct age—*by last birthday.*

Examiner says: "Lay pencils down! Before you begin I will show you exactly what you are to do. Let us read the directions." Examiner then reads aloud the instructions on the front page, while the pupils read silently. Examiner then asks if all understand. If some do not understand, repeat as much as is necessary.

Examiner now says: "Open your booklets to Exercise 1, and turn the opposite page under like this." (Demonstrate. The pictures of Exercise 6 which appear upside down on page opposite Exercise 1 are then out of sight.) "You see that there are 3 problems in Exercise 1 all like the sample test on the front cover which we have just looked at; do them all in the same way. When you have finished Exercise 1, turn the page over and do Exercise 2, then Exercise 3, then Exercise 4, and so on until you have tried them all. If you don't know the right answers, guess. Write one letter in each square."

Repeat privately any instructions necessary. Each child must understand what he is asked to do. No child is expected to answer *all* the questions correctly, but he should try them all. Examiner must see that answers are being plainly written in the proper place; that is, in the blank spaces provided in the margins.

Time: Allow 45 minutes if necessary. Booklets are handed in as soon as finished, but examiner should be careful not to imply by word or manner that this is a speed test. The intention is to give all the time desired by 95 per cent of pupils.

INSTRUCTIONS FOR GIVING TEST II

Pupils must be seated so as to prevent copying.

Desks are cleared and monitors pass out booklets, one to each pupil.

Examiner instructs all pupils to fill in properly the heading blanks, being particulaily careful to obtain correct age—*by last birthday.*

DIRECTIONS FOR EXERCISE 1

Examiner says: "Lay pencils down. Before you begin I will show you exactly what you are to do. Turn to Exercise 1. Let us read the directions." Examiner reads aloud, and pupils silently, the directions for Exercise 1 printed in test booklet. Examiner must read slowly and point out "picture T" and "picture H" while holding booklet up before class. Examiner must also point out where letters T and H are written in the space for the answers. As soon as all the pupils understand what they are to do, say: "Ready—begin." At the end of 10 minutes, or when all have finished,[1] say: "Stop. Lay pencils down."

DIRECTIONS FOR EXERCISE 2

"Turn to Exercise 2. Let us read the directions: 'Look at Figure 1 on opposite page, and answer as many of the questions below as you can. Answer each question with a single letter. If you don't know, guess.' When you have finished Figure 1, do the same for Figure 2, Figure 3, and Figure 4. If you don't know what to do, raise your hand." As before, instructions are repeated, if necessary, until all understand what is wanted. When all understand, examiner says: "Ready—begin." Allow 18 minutes. At the end of this time, or when all have finished,[1] examiner says: "Stop. Turn to Exercise 3."

DIRECTIONS FOR EXERCISE 3

Section A. "Look at the machine parts on the page opposite Exercise 3; now look at Figure 1 and Figure 2 in Exercise 3. Find where each machine part belongs in Figure 1 or in Figure 2. For example: part A belongs at 1 in Figure 1 or in Figure 2; so A is written beside 1 in the space for the answers." (Point to pulley A and to the pulleys numbered 1 in the two figures so that all may see the correspondence.) "Part W belongs at 2 in Figure 1 or in Figure 2; so W is written beside 2 in the space for the answers." (Point to pulley W and to pulleys 2.) "In the same way find which of the machine parts belong at 3, 4, 5, etc., in Figure 1 or in Figure 2, and write the letters opposite these numbers." Allow 10 minutes.

Section B. "Now read all the questions in Section B and answer as many of them as you can. If you are not sure, guess. When you have finished, hand in your booklet." Allow 12 minutes.

As the nature of this test is somewhat unusual, the examiner must make sure that the pupils understand what is required of them, and for this reason directions may be repeated, or given privately to any pupil who does not understand. The examiner must not, of course, indicate or suggest what is the correct answer in any case, when repeating instructions. Examiner should see that answers are being written in the proper place.

DIRECTIONS FOR SCORING

These tests have been carefully planned to permit of rapid and accurate scoring. All answers are designedly placed at the extreme right-hand margin for each exercise, to facilitate easy checking of answers.

All answers are either right or wrong.

To find the number of correct answers, place the closed test booklet face up on the cardboard key, allowing the latter to project at the right-hand edge sufficiently to expose list of correct answers for Exercise 1; now open booklet to Exercise 1 and check off, with ink or blue pencil, each right answer, counting as

---

[1] If they finish before time is up.

they are checked. Write the number of correct responses at the foot of the column. Then turn to Exercise 2 without removing booklet, pulling the booklet slightly over to the left on the key to expose list of correct answers for Exercise 2, and continue checking and counting the right answers as before. Do the same for all the exercises. Then copy the exercise scores on to the front page and add to find the Total Score. Then fill in the corresponding T-Score from table. In the case of Test I the booklet is reversed to correct Exercises 4, 5, and 6. The scoring can be done very rapidly and accurately by any teacher or competent clerk.